MONTREAL PHOTOS

BY S. E. MCKENZIE

Copyright © 2017 S. E. McKenzie
All rights reserved.
ISBN-13: 978-1-77281-042-4

DEDICATION
To everyone who would like to lose themselves in the splendor of Montreal.

CONTENTS

CONTENTS 1
SNOWY STREET 3
MAISONNEUVE GUARDING 4
NOTRE DAMME BASCILLA 4
MAISONNEUVE ON AN ICY DAY 5
ONE OF MANY TUNNELS UNDER THE CITY 6
TUNNEL WALKER 7
WALKING UNDERGROUND 8
CONNECTING TUNNELS UNDER THE CITY 9
SQUIRREL CLIMBING ABOVE 10
THE SNOW BELOW 10
SQUIRREL IN SNOW 11
AN APPLE A DAY 12
DOG SLEIGH 13
MONUMENT TO 14
PAUL CHOMEDEY DE MAISONNEUVE 14
FOUNTAIN 15
IN THE WORLD TRADE CENTRE MONTREAL 15
ANOTHER LOOK AT THE FOUNTAIN 16
WORLD TRADE CENTRE 17
SMOKE 18
SNOW FESTIVAL 19
ANOTHER VIEW OF THE SNOW FESTIVAL 20
THE FRENCH POODLE 21
ANOTHER VIEW OF THE FRENCH POODLE 22
STAIRWAY IN PLACE VICTORIA 23
OLYMPIC FLAME 24
THE ENGISH PUG 25

S.E. McKENZIE

THE ENGLISH PUG ANOTHER VIEW	26
SAD HORSE	27
REMEMBERANCE	28
PRAYER	29
UNITY AT REMEMBERANCE SERVICE	30
NOTRE DAME BASCILLA	31
MONUMENT TO ADMIRAL NELSON	32
SCENIC WALK ALONG THE PORT	33
OUTSIDE THE NATIONAL BANK BUILDING	34
A CLOSER VIEW OF THE TREE	35
ANOTHER GREAT DOOR	36
TO THE FINANCIAL DISTRICT	36
MAURICE RICHARD (The Rocket)	37

MONTREAL: Photos

SNOWY STREET

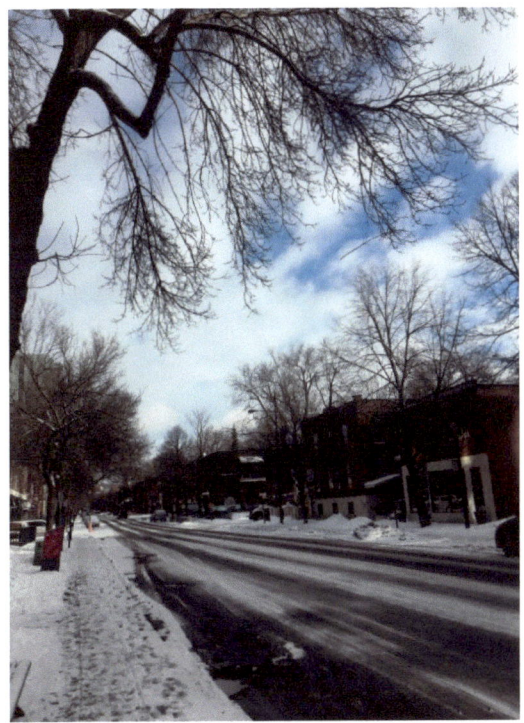

S.E. McKenzie

MAISONNEUVE GUARDING NOTRE DAMME BASCILLA

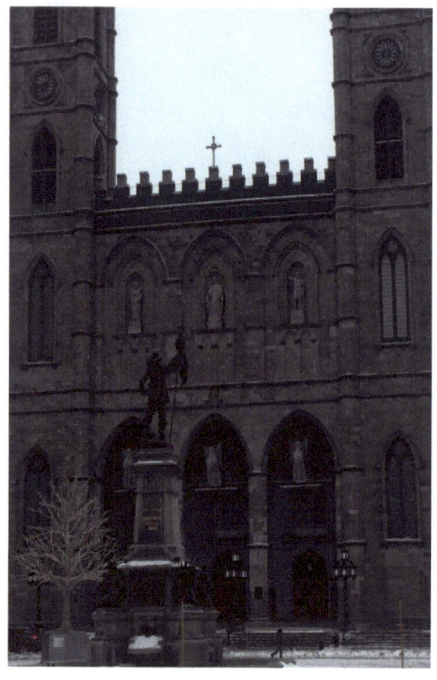

MONTREAL: Photos

MAISONNEUVE ON AN ICY DAY

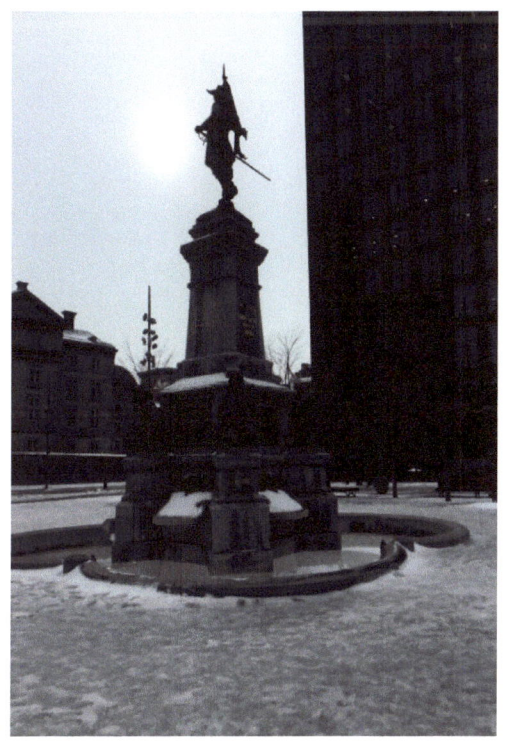

S.E. McKENZIE

ONE OF MANY TUNNELS UNDER THE CITY

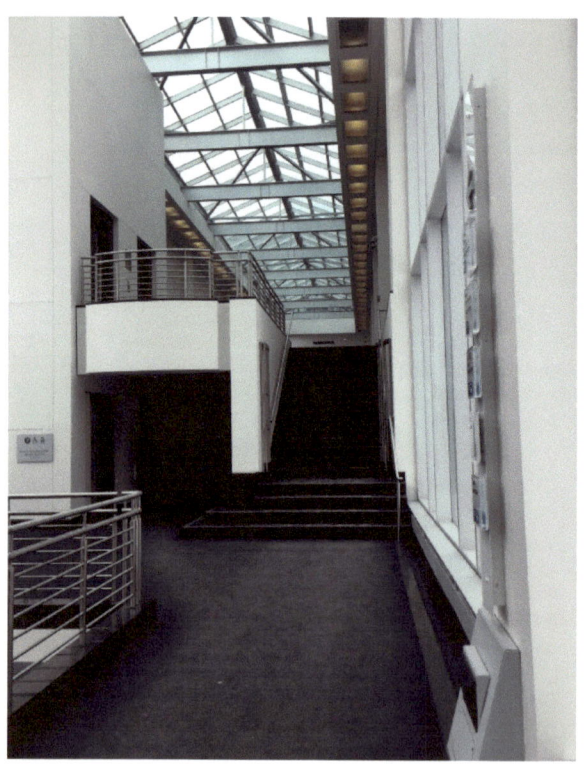

MONTREAL: Photos

TUNNEL WALKER

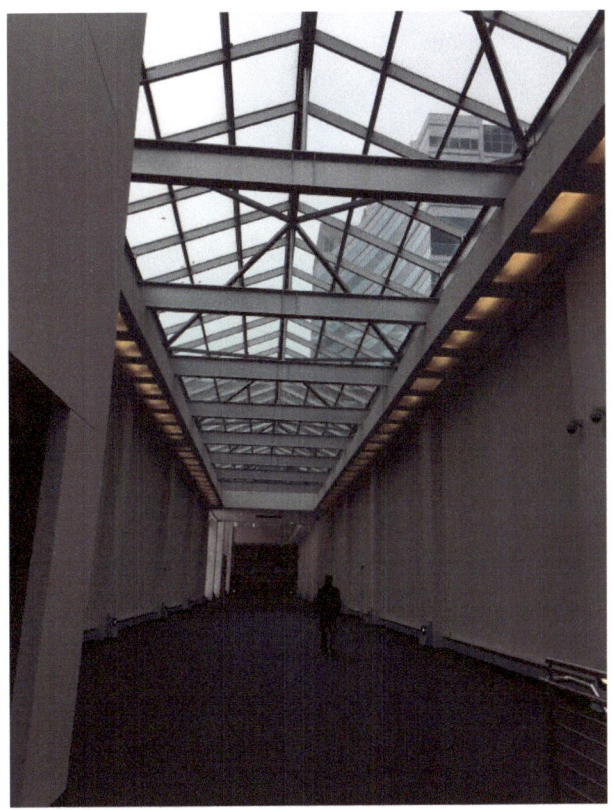

S.E. McKENZIE

WALKING UNDERGROUND

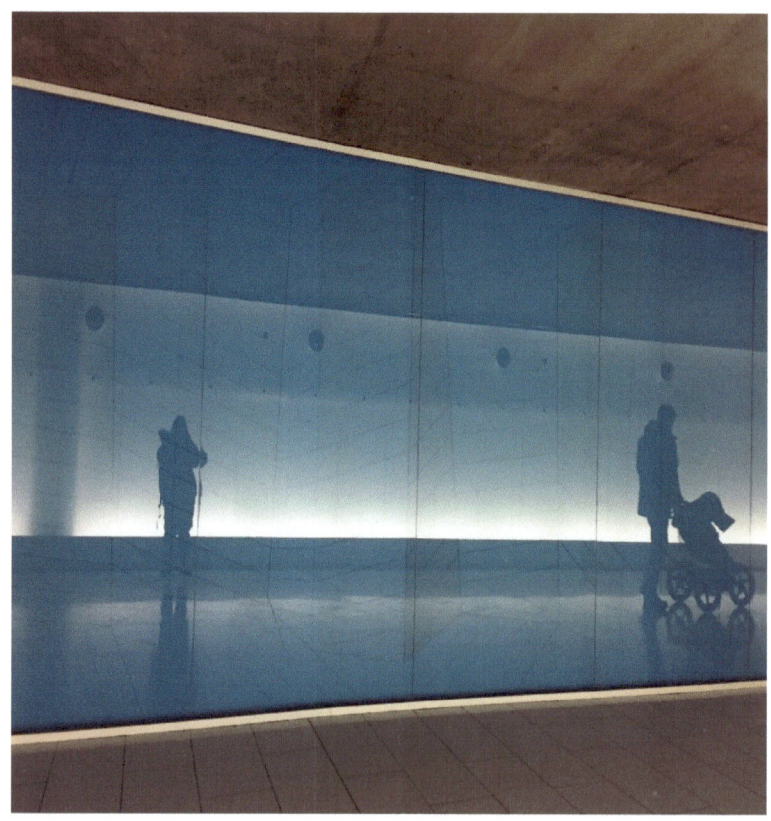

MONTREAL: Photos

CONNECTING TUNNELS UNDER THE CITY

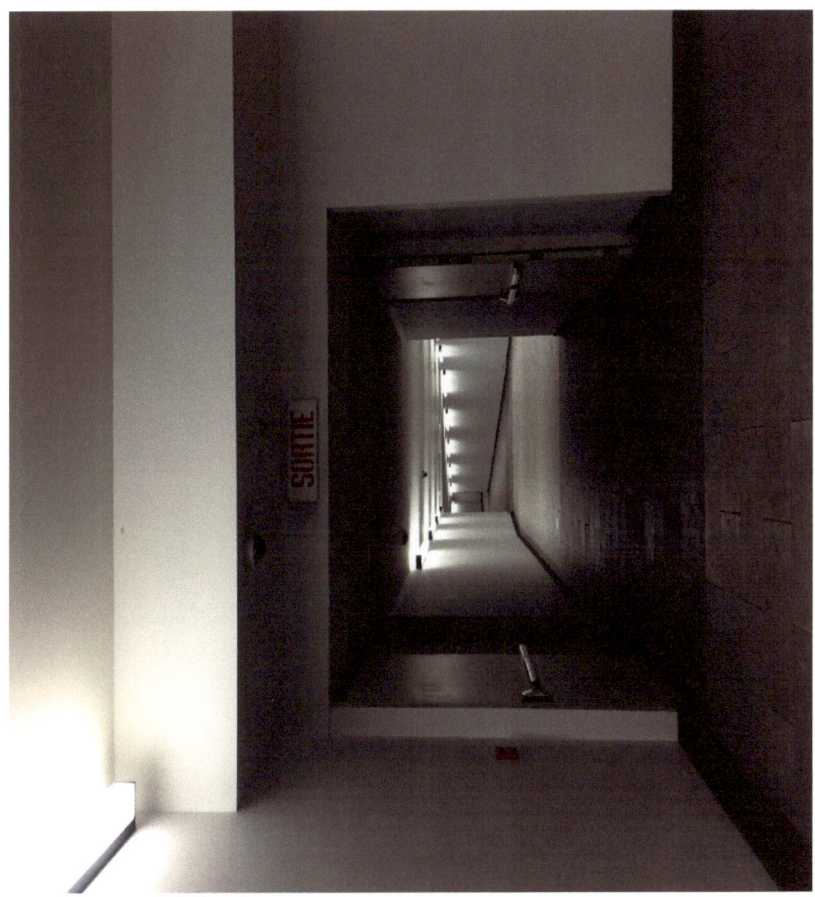

S.E. McKENZIE

SQUIRREL CLIMBING ABOVE
THE SNOW BELOW

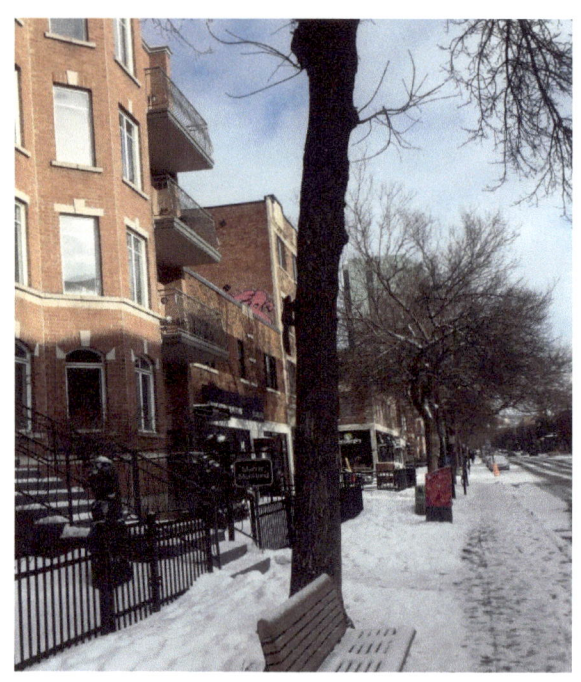

MONTREAL: Photos

SQUIRREL IN SNOW

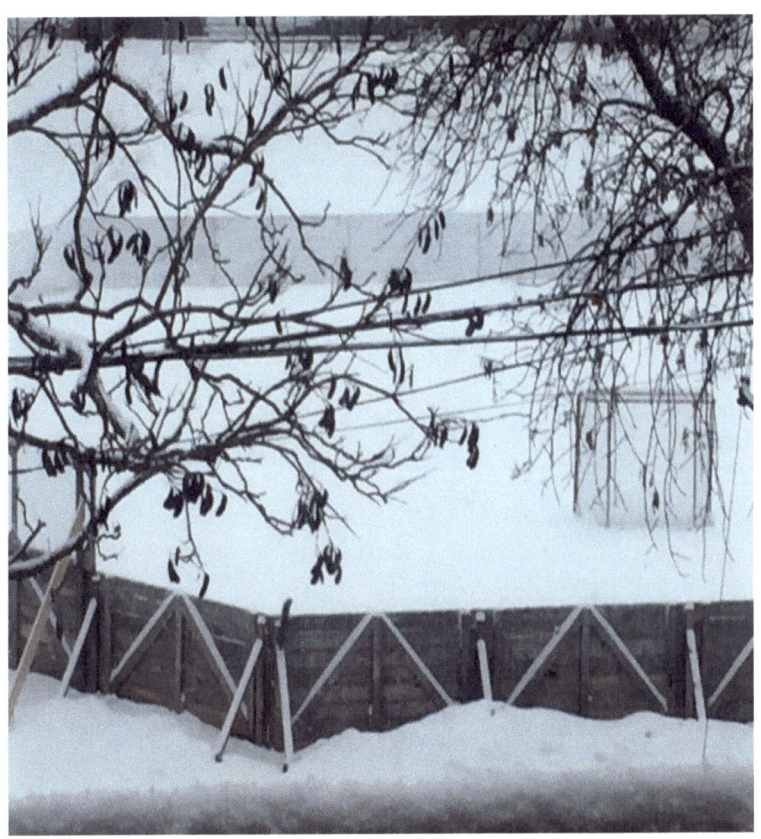

AN APPLE A DAY

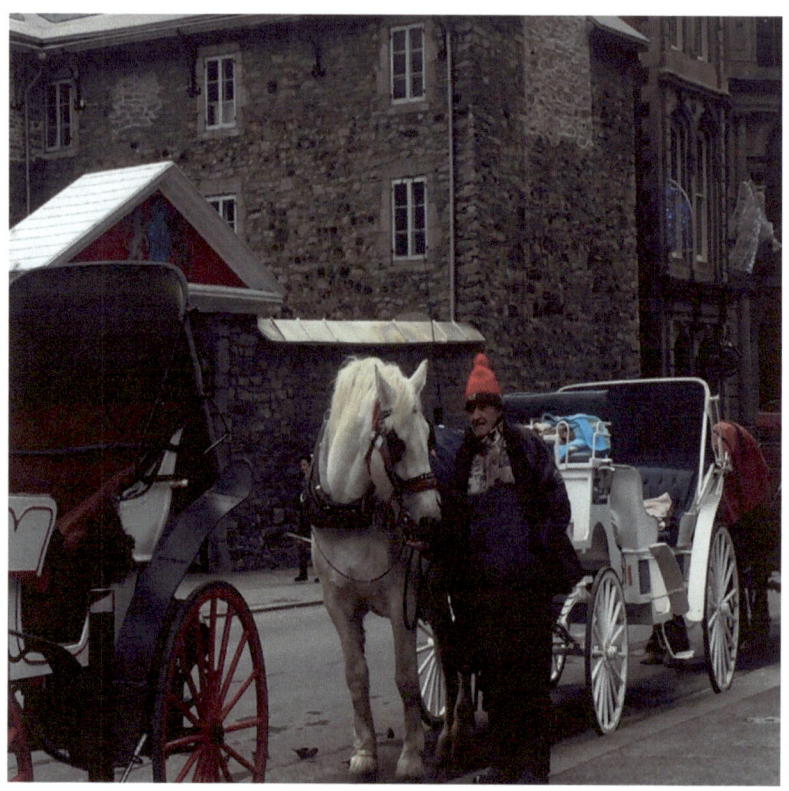

MONTREAL: Photos

DOG SLEIGH

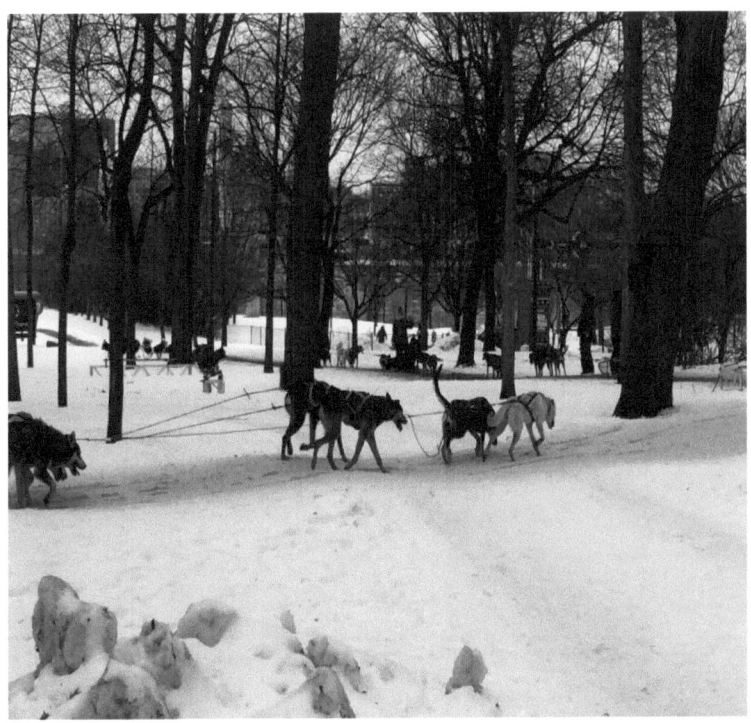

S.E. McKENZIE

MONUMENT TO
PAUL CHOMEDEY DE MAISONNEUVE

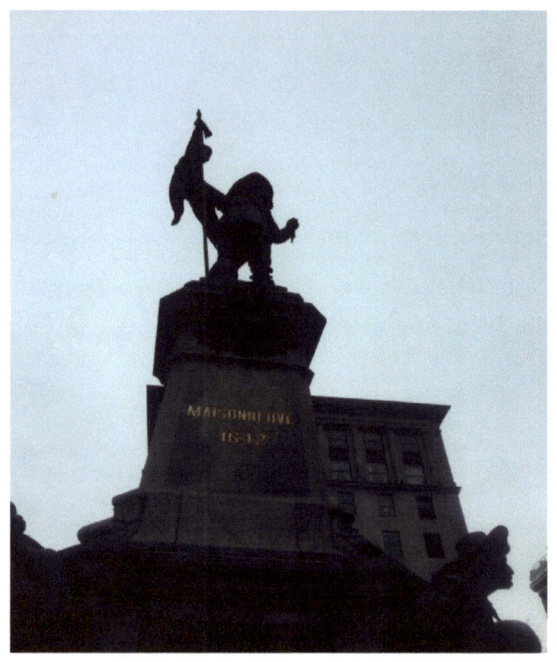

MONTREAL: Photos

FOUNTAIN
IN THE WORLD TRADE CENTRE MONTREAL

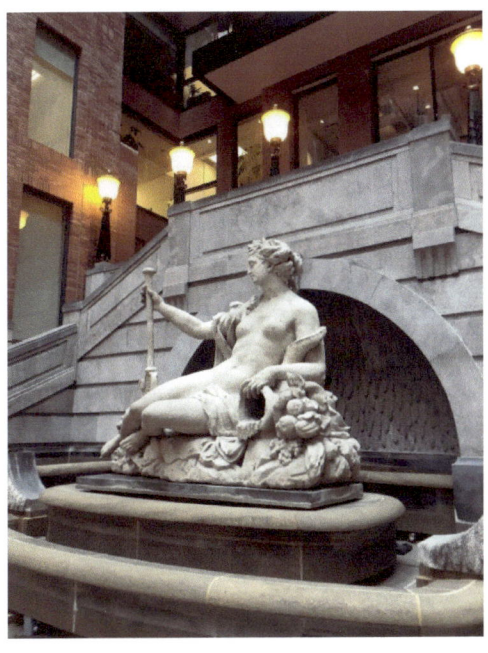

S.E. McKENZIE

ANOTHER LOOK AT THE FOUNTAIN

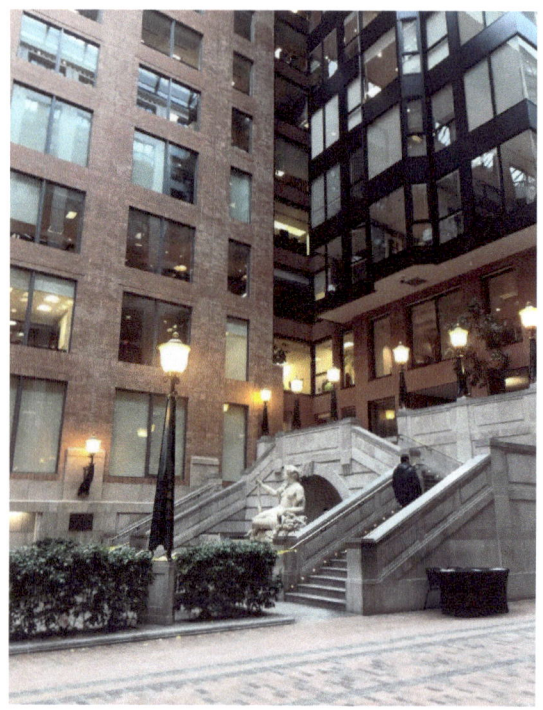

MONTREAL: Photos

WORLD TRADE CENTRE

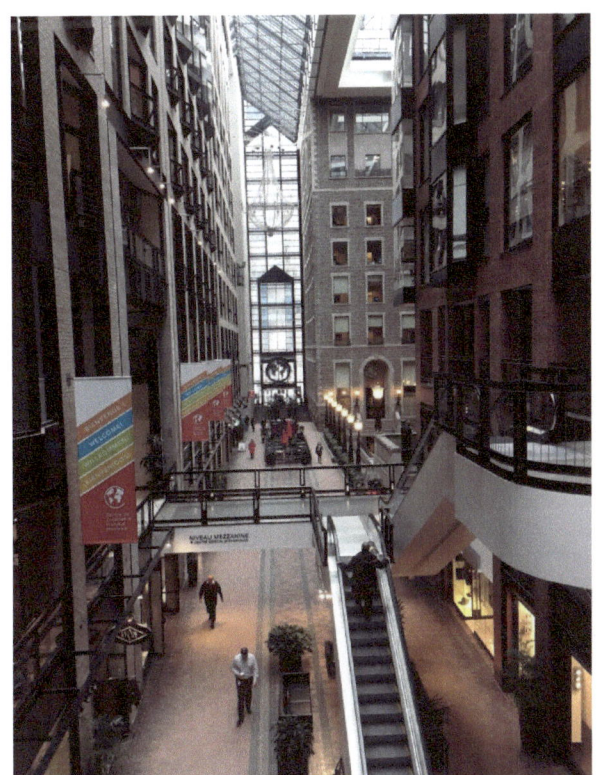

O

SMOKE

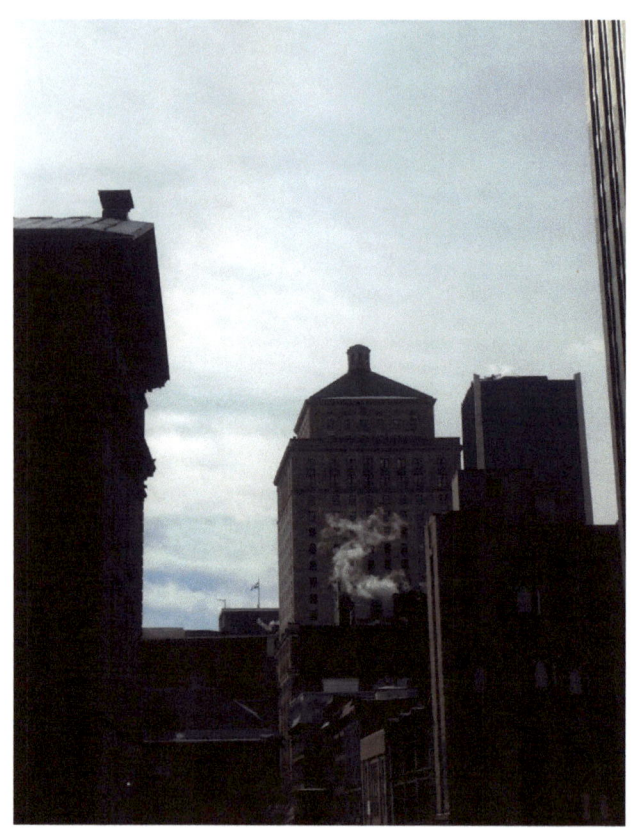

MONTREAL: Photos

SNOW FESTIVAL

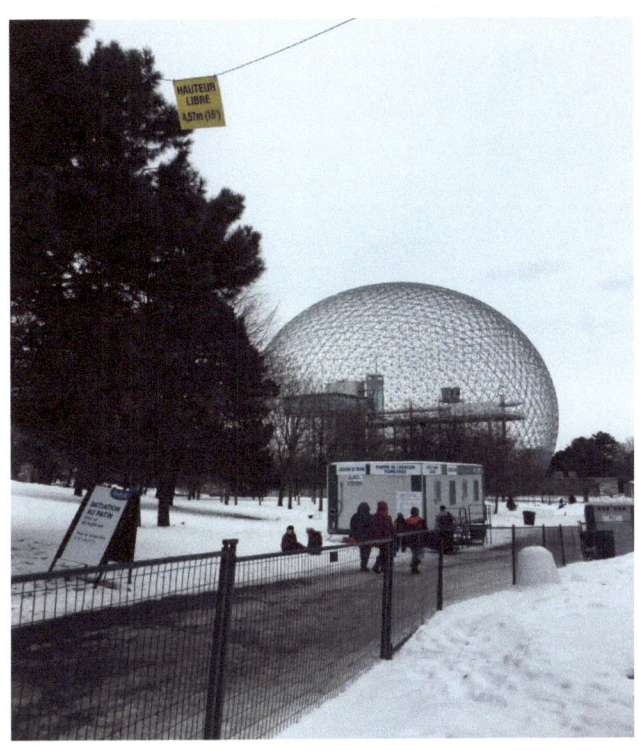

ANOTHER VIEW OF THE SNOW FESTIVAL

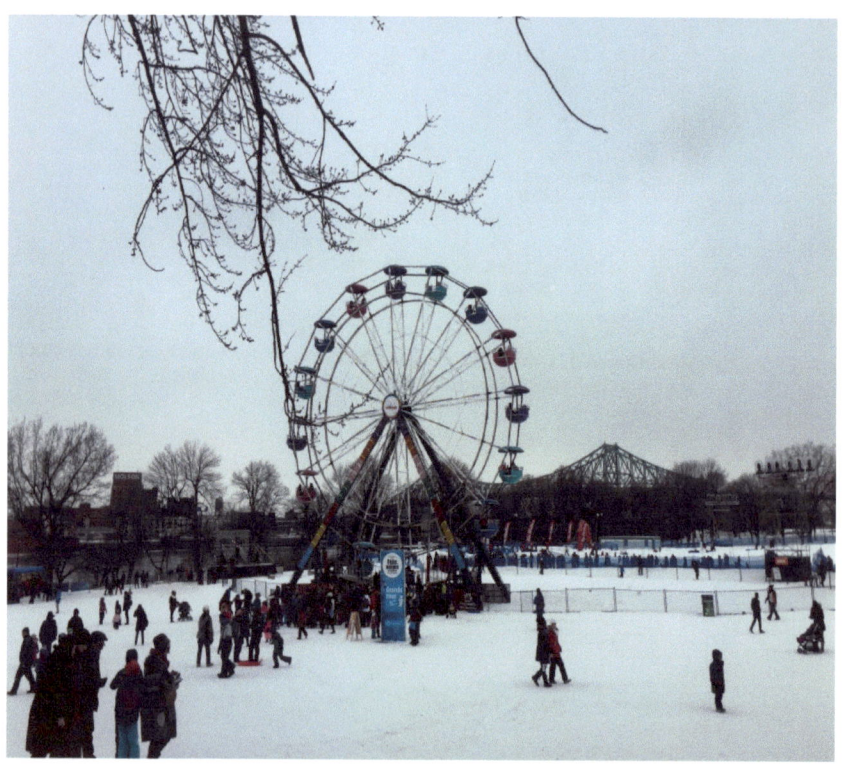

MONTREAL: Photos

THE FRENCH POODLE

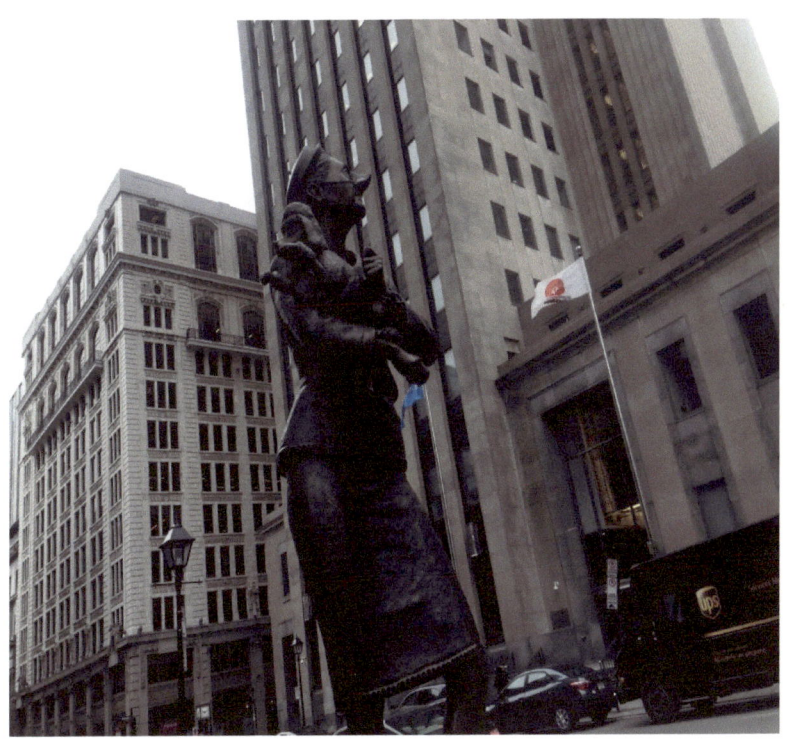

S.E. McKENZIE

ANOTHER VIEW OF THE FRENCH POODLE

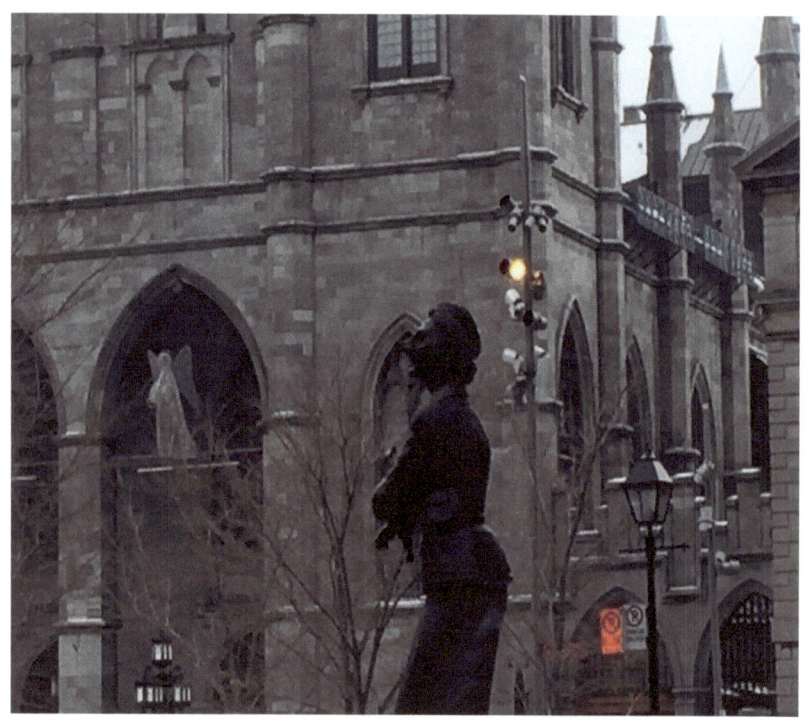

MONTREAL: Photos

STAIRWAY IN PLACE VICTORIA

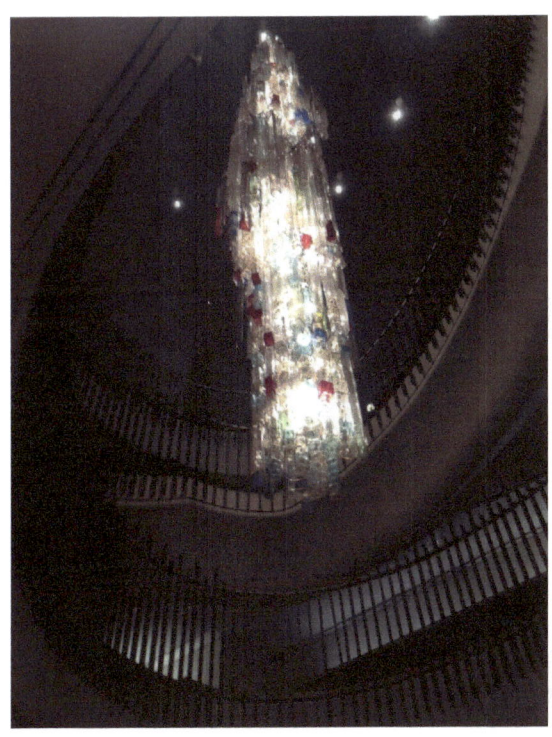

OLYMPIC FLAME

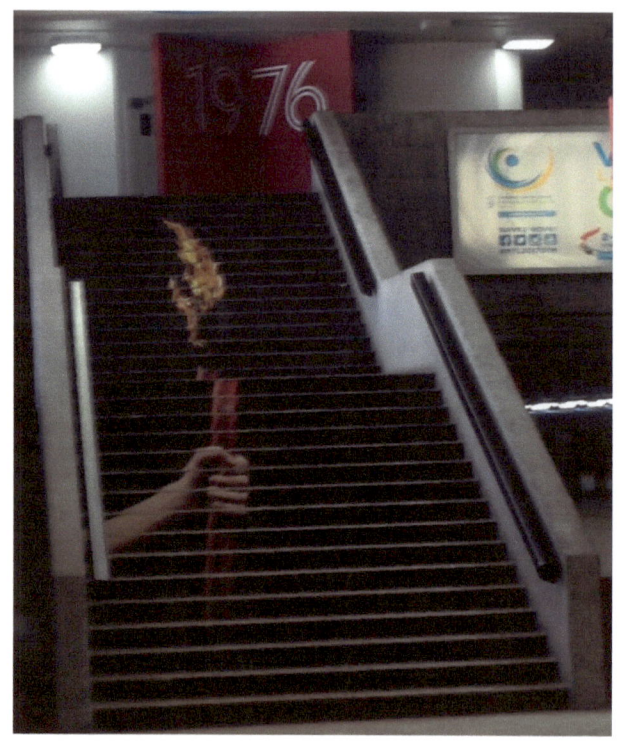

MONTREAL: Photos

THE ENGISH PUG

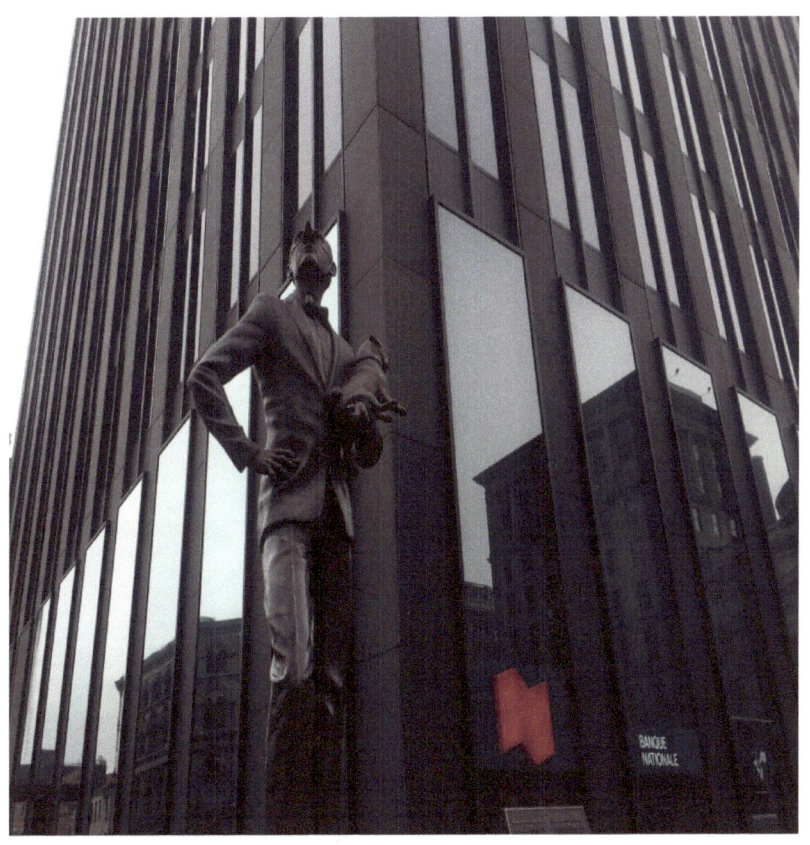

S.E. McKENZIE

THE ENGLISH PUG ANOTHER VIEW

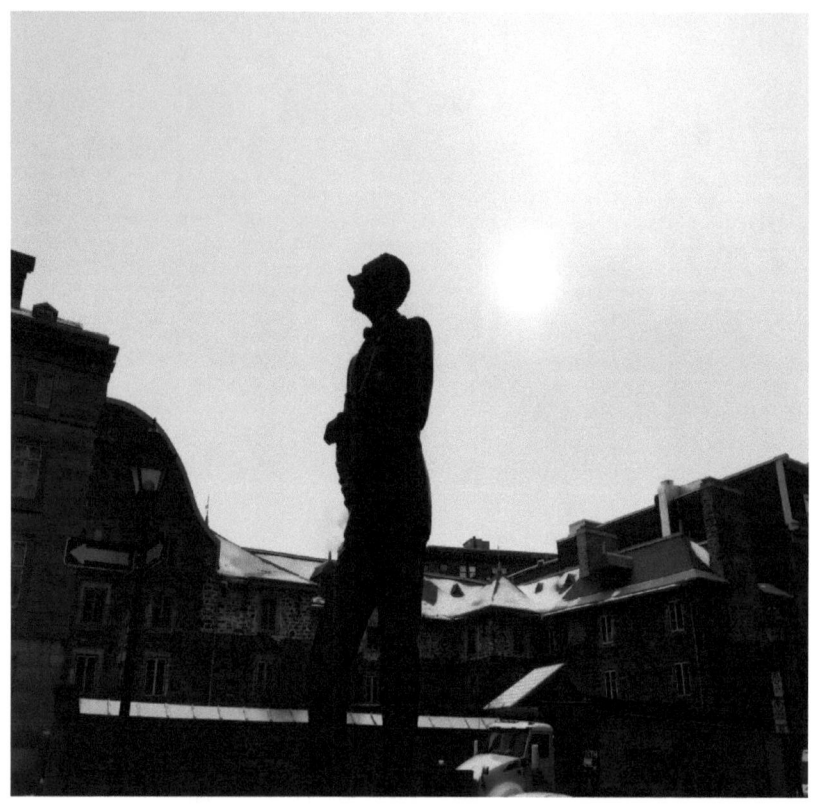

MONTREAL: Photos

SAD HORSE

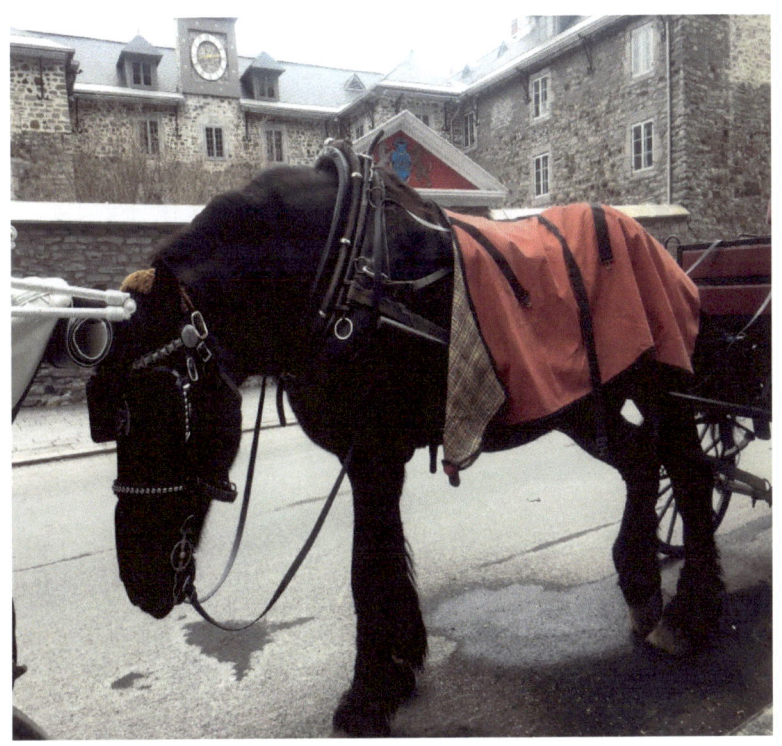

S.E. McKENZIE

REMEMBERANCE

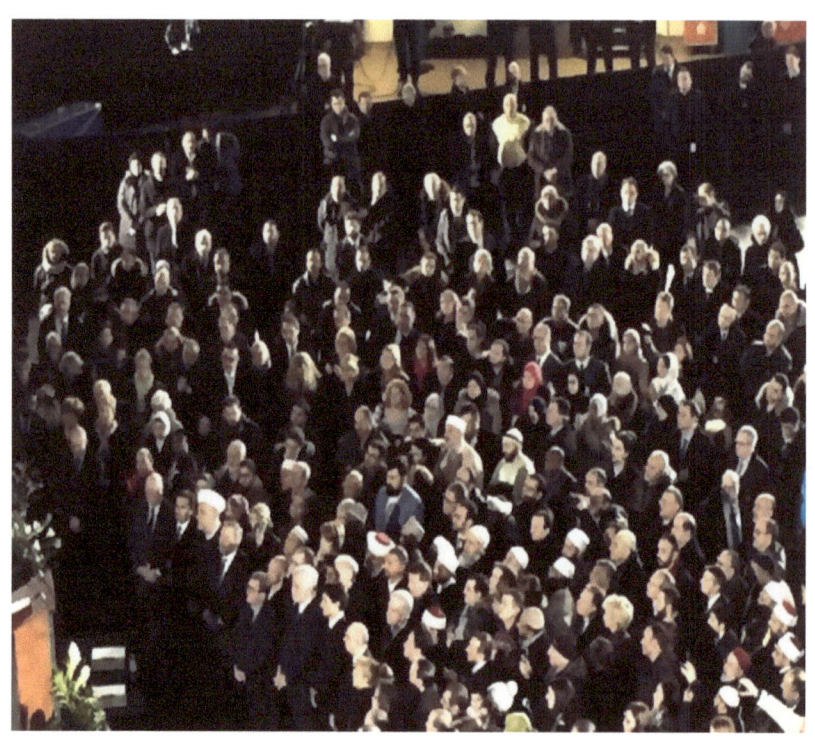

MONTREAL: Photos

PRAYER

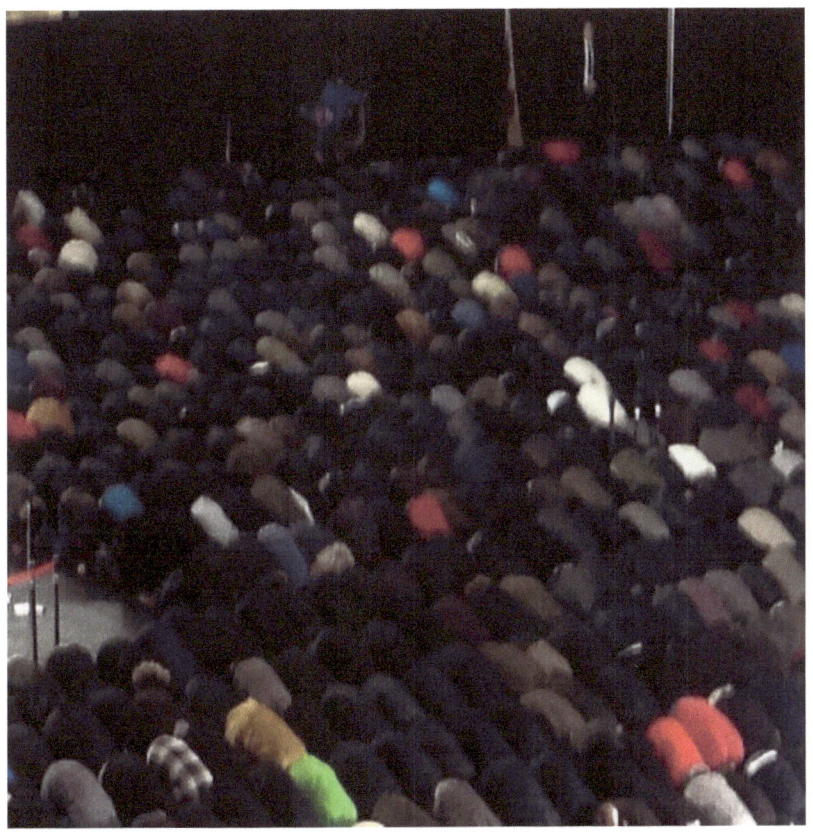

S.E. McKENZIE

UNITY AT REMEMBERANCE SERVICE

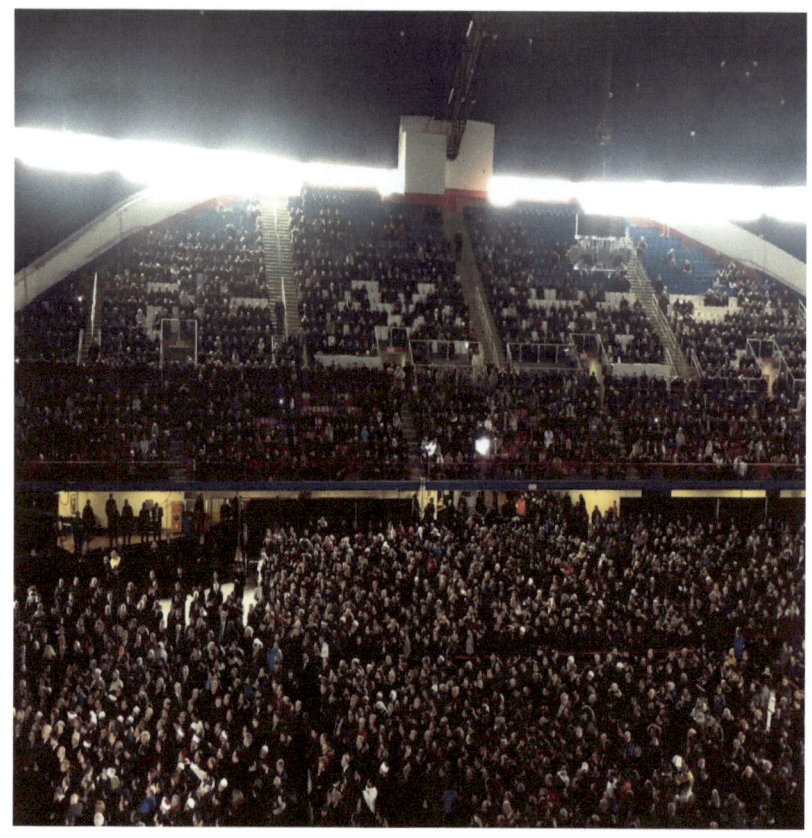

MONTREAL: Photos

NOTRE DAME BASCILLA

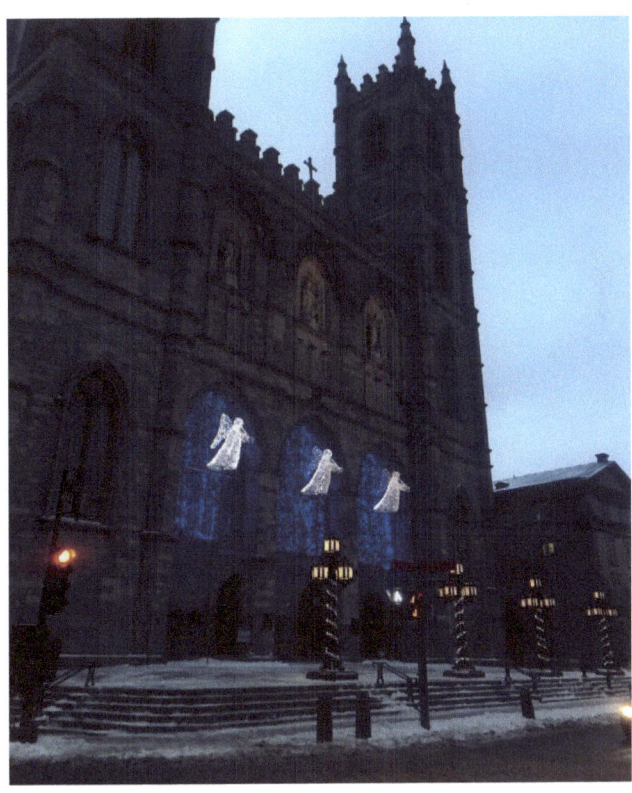

S.E. McKENZIE

MONUMENT TO ADMIRAL NELSON

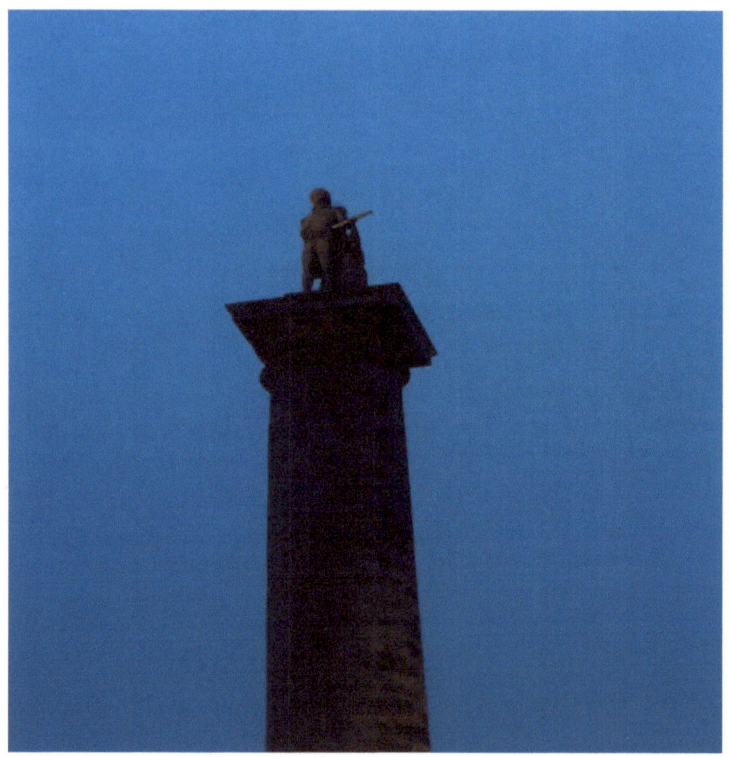

MONTREAL: Photos

SCENIC WALK ALONG THE PORT

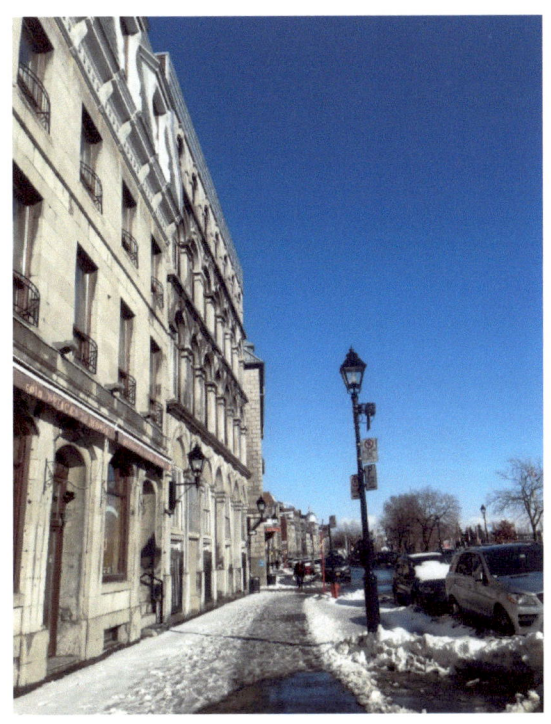

S.E. McKENZIE

OUTSIDE THE NATIONAL BANK BUILDING

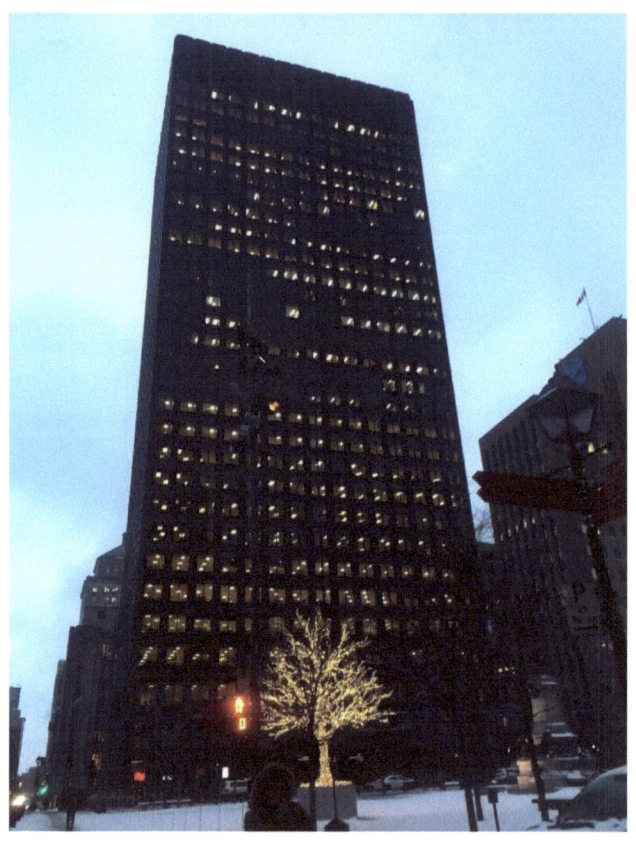

MONTREAL: Photos

A CLOSER VIEW OF THE TREE

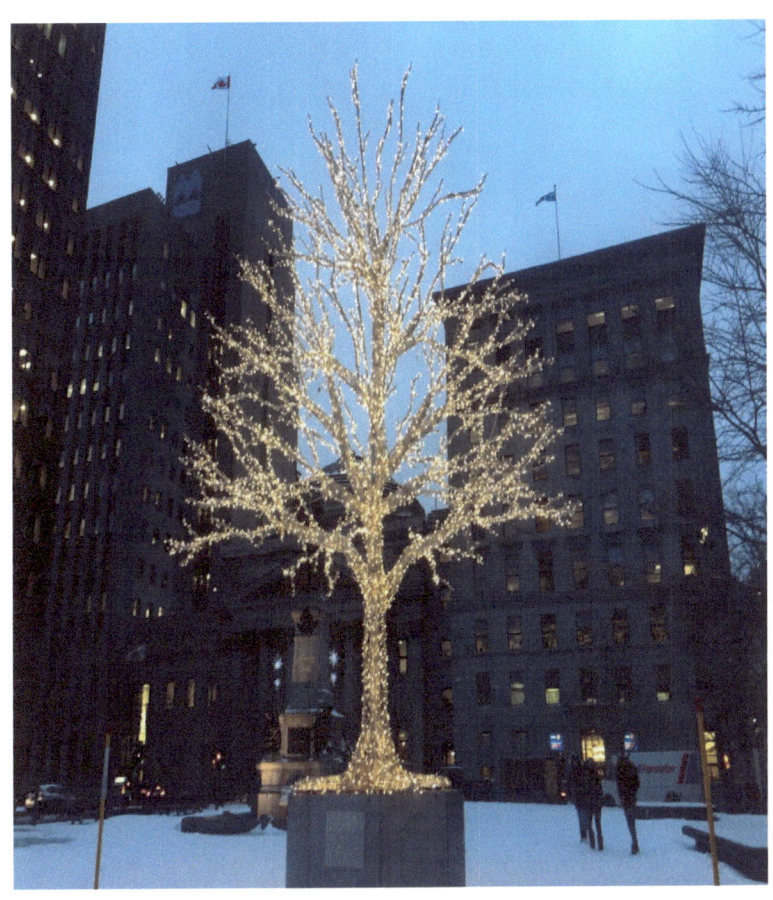

S.E. McKENZIE

ANOTHER GREAT DOOR
TO THE FINANCIAL DISTRICT

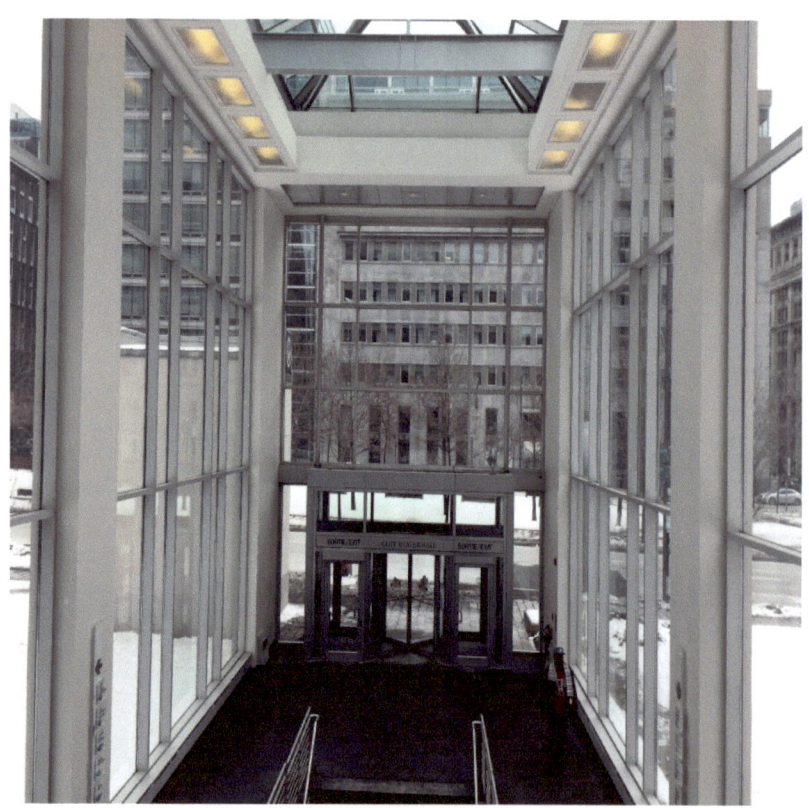

MONTREAL: Photos

MAURICE RICHARD (The Rocket)

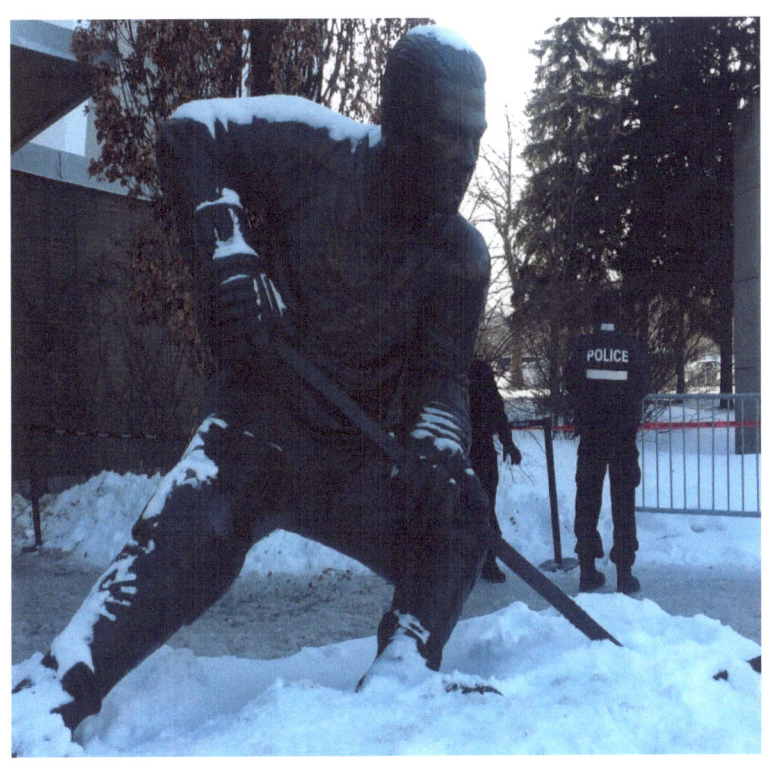

THE END

Produced by S.E. McKenzie Productions
First Print Edition 2017

Copyright © 2017 by S. E. McKenzie
All rights reserved.

Email:
messidartha@aol.com

http://www.amazon.com/SarahMcKenzie/e/B00H9RWX48/

www.ingramcontent.com/pod-product-compliance
Lightning Source LLC
Chambersburg PA
CBHW040251220526
45473CB00001B/444

Mana Sciences™

THE SCIENCE of IMAGINATION

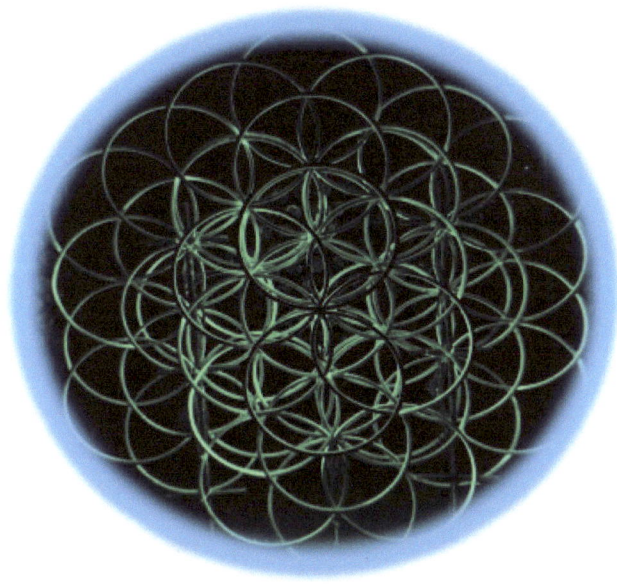

Michelle Shine, Ph.D.
& Keti Kamalani

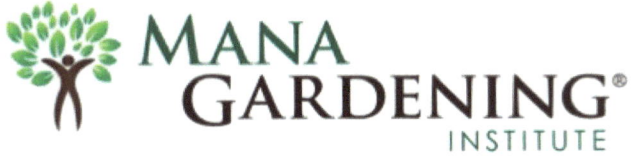

Dedicated to advancing the Hawaiian art of personal empowerment for the mind, body & spirit.

Published by Mana Gardening Institute, LLC, Kaneohe, Hawaii. Copyright 2018 by Keti Kamalani and Michelle Shine, Ph.D. All rights reserved. No part of this publication may be reproduced, stored in a retrieval system, or Transmitted in any form or by any means electronic, mechanical, photocopying, recorded or otherwise without the prior written permission of the authors except in the case of "fair use" as brief quotations used in reviews or articles. For permissions please write to: Mana Gardening Institute, LLC 48-145 Waiahole Homestead Road, Kaneohe, Hawaii 96744. The DNA image appearing before chapter 1 is a public domain image. All other photographs appearing in this book are copyrighted original photographs of Mana Gardening Institute. The authors and publisher of this book do not dispense medical or health advice or prescribe the use of any technique as a form of treatment for physical or medical problems without the advice of a physician, either directly or indirectly. Should you use any of the information in this book, the authors and publisher assume no responsibility for your actions. Cover designs by Mana Gardening Institute, LLC.
Www.ManaGardening.com

Contents

1. Vision & Intention of this Book
2. Introduction: What is Mana Gardening & Hawaiian Empowerment?
3. What You Imagine is Real
4. Imaginary Exercising has Real Biological Effects
5. Enhanced Performance from Imagining
6. What is Happening When Imagining Being Touched?
7. Imagination has Real Psychological Effects
8. The Power of Belief & the Placebo Effect
9. Improved Intuition through Imagination
10. Creation through Imagination
11. Conclusion: You Are A Powerful Creator!
12. Guided Meditation: Imagine your Sacred Inner Garden

References

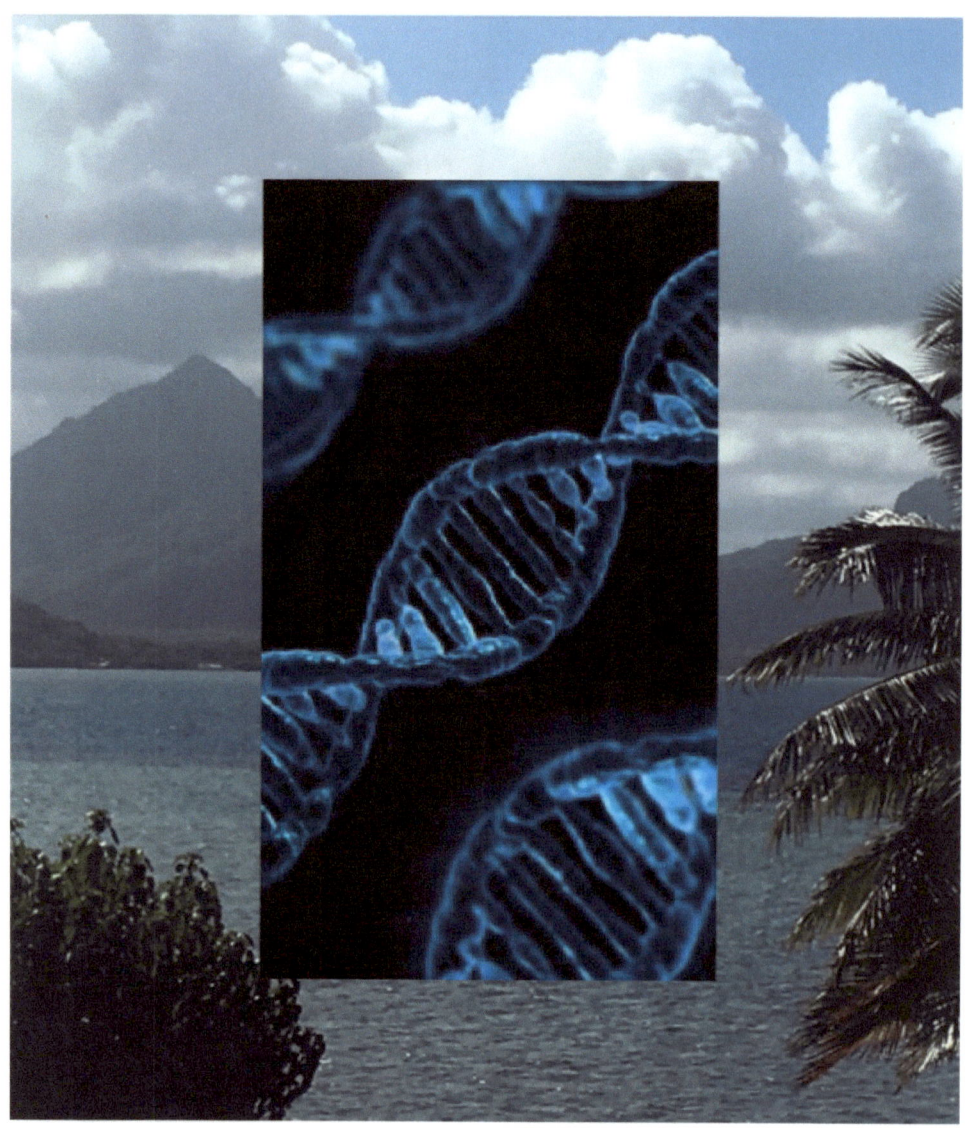

1~ Vision & Intention of this Book

The intention of this Mana Sciences™ publication is to share scientific data that support the Hawaiian mindfulness practices of imagination described here and in our full-length book, *Mana Gardening, Empower Yourself & Live a Better Life*.

This guidebook shares the physical and psychological benefits Keti and I experienced from using these inward techniques. and is designed to give you an easy-to-understand grasp of the research data with concise summaries of the findings that support its efficacy. Perhaps these data will encourage you to try the profound, Hawaiian empowerment techniques for yourself. At the end of this book, there is a participatory guided meditation that allows you to have your own inner experience of your potent imagination.

Our vision is that through reading this you realize on a deeper level that you are more powerful and creative than you previously considered.

Our hope is that you begin *Mana Gardening* on your own and enjoy a better, more creative life!

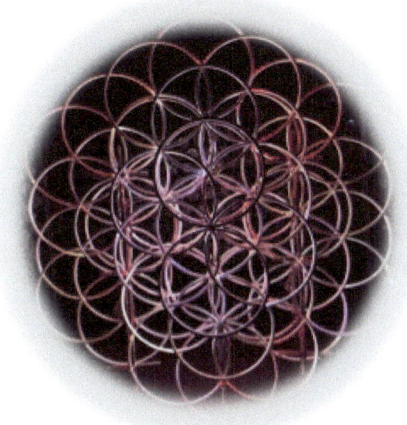

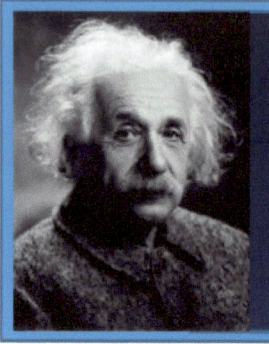

"Imagination is everything. It is the preview to life's coming attractions"
-Albert Einstein

2~ Introduction: What is Mana Gardening & Hawaiian Empowerment?

Ancient Hawaiians discovered the secrets of empowerment from within. They call this power *Mana*. Hawaiian *Mana Gardening* is a unique, relaxing and quick method of going inward using your potent imagination. The idea is to imagine your personal paradise and use that as a starting point to relax deeply, feel great peace and fulfillment, and access your inner wisdom and creativity. Keti and I call this inner imaginary space, *the inner garden*. With practice, you will find that you are able to create what you want to see in the world using these techniques.

Consistent *Mana Gardening* guides you to know clearly and concisely what you want, what you need, and what is the best path forward for you. Aligning your mind, body and soul, these Hawaiian personal empowerment techniques help you to feel energized, or relaxed, as wanted or needed, anytime, anywhere. Our book, *Mana Gardening, Empower Yourself & Live a Better Life* shares our story and guides you inward to your own inner garden so that you may begin to create a life you absolutely love.

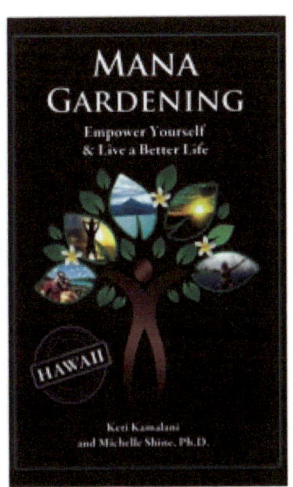

Quotes

*"What you imagine on the inside
can be created on the outside,
in real life."*

*"Your body believes you; it reacts to
whatever you believe."*

*"What you imagine, believe,
or perceive to be true
is real
on biological and psychological levels."*

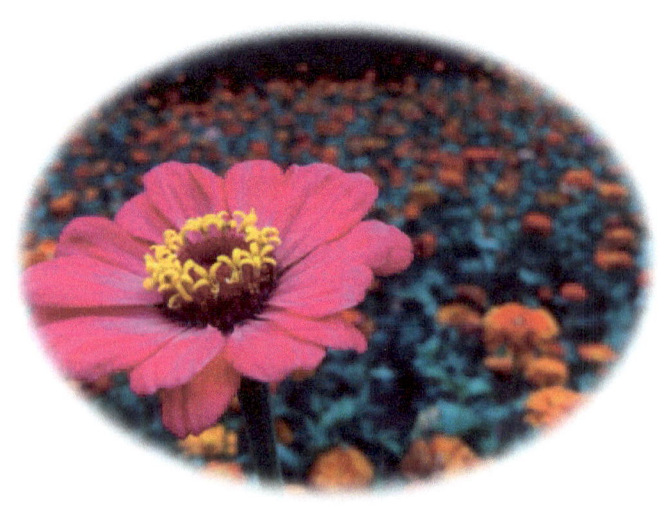

3~ What You Imagine is Real

"Seek first the Kingdom," the Hawaiian healer said to me, but, unlike the rest of the wise souls I encountered, he did not ask me to search for anything; he guided me to look inside to my own personal heaven or paradise. That imaginary yet energetic space that we call the inner garden is, in many ways, the essence of creation.

What you imagine on the inside can then be created on the outside, in real life. Imagine happiness, create happiness; imagine relaxation, create relaxation; imagine being better at something, and be better at it; imagine healthy, loving, supportive relationships, and have them. Keti and I saw this firsthand. Our thoughts, visualizations, beliefs, and perspectives profoundly changed our lives, not just emotionally, but physically too.

Keti and I practiced this technique for over 10 years with profound results giving us a feeling of being empowered from within. In Hawaiian, *Mana* is the life force energy that flows through all things. Using these ancient Hawaiian mindfulness techniques, this *Mana* flows to us and through us, benefitting us and everyone we know in countless ways. The *Mana Gardening* series of books was written due to our enthusiasm over our experiences.

As biomedical research scientists, we searched the primary literature and sought out what fellow researchers were uncovering that may provide a basis for the exciting physical and psychological benefits we were receiving from consistently going within to experience our own inner gardens.

We are delighted to have an opportunity to share these scientific discoveries on imagination with you and trust that the findings reported here will motivate you to enjoy some time *Mana Gardening* every day.

In researching the powerful effects of imagination, we came across numerous studies suggesting that what you imagine *is real* on a biological level. Research shows that mental imagery, which is the type of imagining you do when *Mana Gardening*, can have measurable, physical effects in real life. These studies reveal how mental imagery affects us in detectable biological ways, such as in brain activation and reorganization, changes in heart rate and blood pressure, and in parameters such as physical performance of tasks.

The first scientific finding might help those who believe they have trouble imagining in general. It has been documented that those who, at first, demonstrate difficulty imagining, eventually report improved ability with practice.[1] Other researchers were able to document this improvement by showing enhanced brain activation with continued mental imagery practice.[2,3] With practice, imagination can improve! These lines of evidence support the idea that visualizing your inner garden will become easier and easier and may have real effects in your brain.

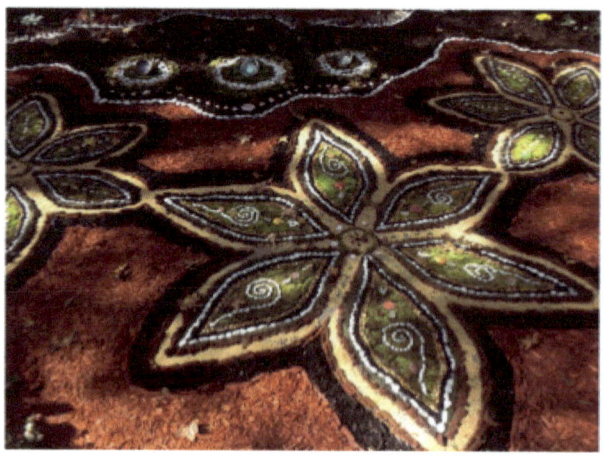

Mental Imagery = Imagining, Visualizing

Creates measurable, physical effects:

- *Brain activation and reorganization*
- *Changes in heart rate*
- *Changes in blood pressure*
- *Changes in respiration rate*
- *Changes in parameters such as physical performance of tasks*

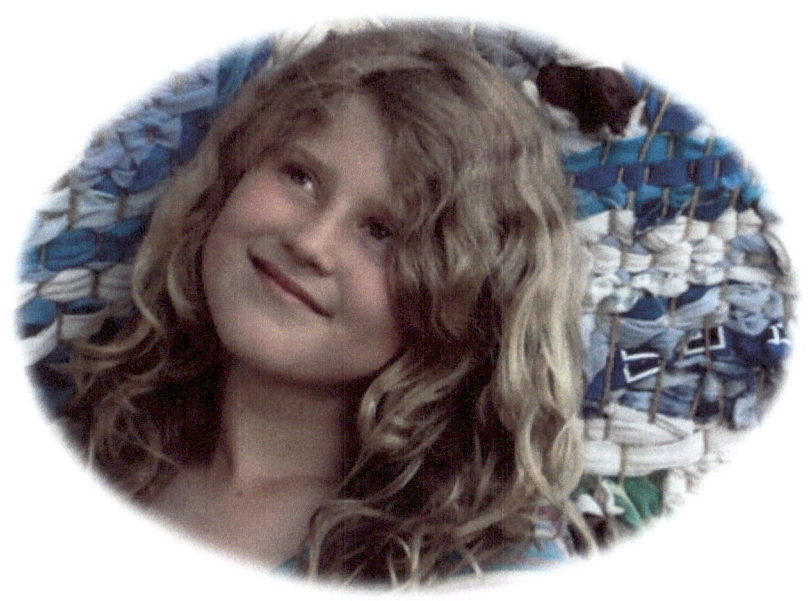

4~ Imaginary Exercising has Real Biological Effects

Many exciting scientific articles validate the possible physical and psychological effects Keti and I were experiencing from consistent *Mana Gardening*. As a distance runner since sixth grade, I find that, besides being great for my body, exercise stabilizes my mood. When I can't make time to work out, I imagine myself trail running in my inner garden (my imaginary paradise or heaven). I visualize myself huffing and puffing up high alpine switchbacks while feeling the exertion of it. After exercising in my inner garden my mood is stabilized for rest of the day and into the next, just like after I run three miles in real life.

That I felt better from simulated exercise was very interesting, so we searched for and discovered many published studies supporting that imaginary exercising can have real physical effects. Data from numerous neurofeedback and functional brain imaging studies indicate that visual motor imagery (which is imaginary exercising or simulated movement) stimulates several areas of the brain in a manner similar to actual movement.[4-13] Furthermore, simulated or imagined movement and actual movement involve overlapping neural structures in the central nervous system.[1-3,6,13-15]

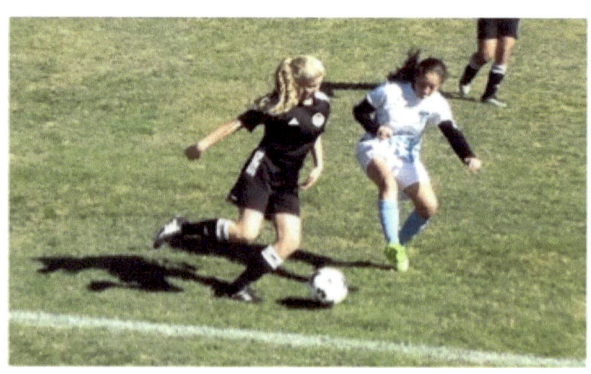

In one particular study, subjects imagined various finger movements (visual motor imagery) combined with pretending to feel the imaginary movements (kinesthetic imagery). Neurofeedback results showed that the motor imagery of imagining the movement combined with kinesthetic imagery of pretending to feel the movements enhanced the activation in certain regions of the brain.[5] Neuroimaging studies also reported increased brain activation when comparing the combination of kinesthetic and visual motor imagery versus motor imagery alone.[2,5]

Besides just the brain being activated by imagination, studies showed that the body also responds to imagination. Basic vital measurements were taken and recorded while healthy subjects walked on a treadmill. Imagining walking on a treadmill at various speeds resulted in similar changes in heart and respiration rates.[16-18]

Let's relate this to imagining trail running in my inner garden. I visualize myself running up the trail while feeling exerted. Since this type of combined imagery (called kinesthetic motor imagery) has been shown in research studies to create brain activations and body reactions similar to what is seen with real movements,[2,5,16-18] then perhaps this is why I feel better after imagining trail running in my inner garden: my body responds as if I really participated in the exercise.

The mental imagery of *Mana Gardening* can activate the brain and body as if physical things are really happening.

Visual Motor Imagery = Imaginary Exercising or Simulated Movement

Neurofeedback and functional brain imaging studies indicate that visual motor imagery:

- *Stimulates several areas of the brain in a manner similar to actual movement [4-13]*

- *In relation to actual movement, involves overlapping neural structures in the central nervous system [1-3,6,13-15]*

- *When combined with kinesthetic imagery (the feeling component) enhances brain activation as compared to motor imagery alone [2-5]*

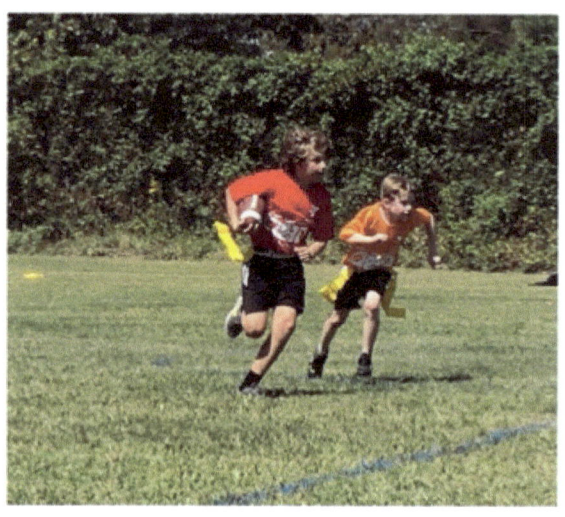

5~ Enhanced Performance from Imagining

Being a very active person, I also enjoy surfing in my inner garden. In real life, before moving away from Hawaii, I enjoyed an improvement in my surfing abilities as my movements became more integrated. I finally felt like a real surfer.

In my inner garden, I had been imagining myself pulling off moves I was not able to do yet in real life while also imagining the feeling of the water underneath my board being pushed by my legs as I made turns. Studies suggest that this form of kinesthetic motor imagery added to surfing in real life once or twice per week, may have enhanced my actual surfing performance.

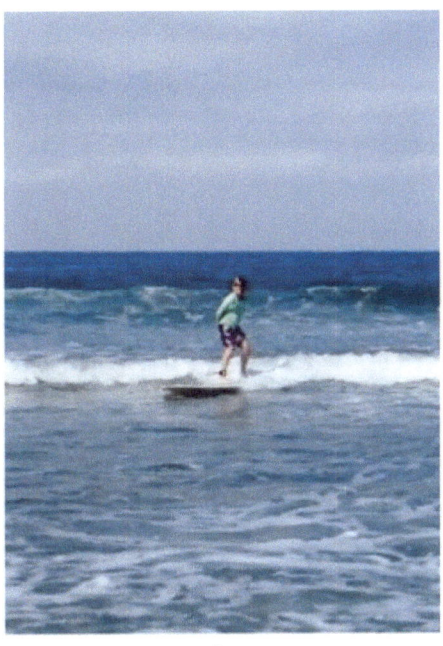

Researchers found that, when learning new tasks, such as dancing steps for the tango, subjects who practiced the steps in their imagination by both visualizing and feeling the movements, for 15 minutes per day, in addition to physical practice, showed expanded brain activation compared to those who practiced only physically. What is more, these subjects also actually performed better than the subjects who did not practice in their imagination.[19] Kinesthetic motor imagery, when used in combination with the corresponding physical activity, can activate and reorganize the brain, and can also improve the physical performance of that activity.[9,20,21] Toward this end, many athletes now use mental imagery (mentally rehearsing movements) as an important part of their training.[8,22-24] Evidence suggests that the imaginary exercise done in the inner garden activates the brain and body, resulting in physical benefits from the imagined experiences.

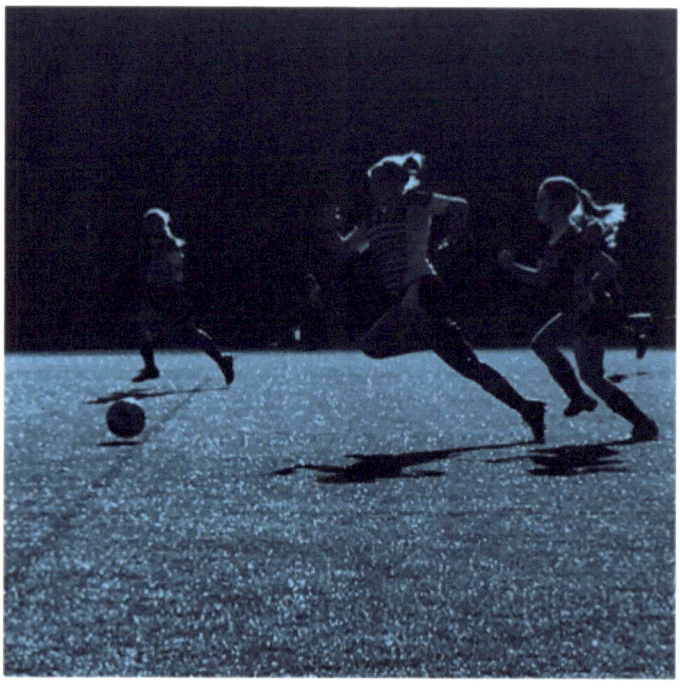

6~ What is Happening When Imagining Being Touched?

Massages are another way I enjoy my inner garden. When I really want to relax, I imagine getting a massage while enjoying serene surroundings of nature. The kinesthetic imagery of feeling the other's hands on my shoulders progressing down my back gives my senses a treat. Immediately, I feel my muscles relax in real life as if a massage therapist had actually touched me. Data was found to support this too.

Researchers found that the mental imagery of touch facilitated tactile processing in the brain.[25] In other words, the brain reacted to the imagined touch as if touch had actually occurred, suggesting that touch imagined through *Mana Gardening* may have real effects in the brain and body. I may have given my body the gift of getting a real massage while simply imagining this experience in the context of my inner garden. Taken together, evidence indicates that imagined experiences cause brain activations and body responses similar to actual events and supports that your imagination can result in real biological effects.

What you imagine is real on a biological level.

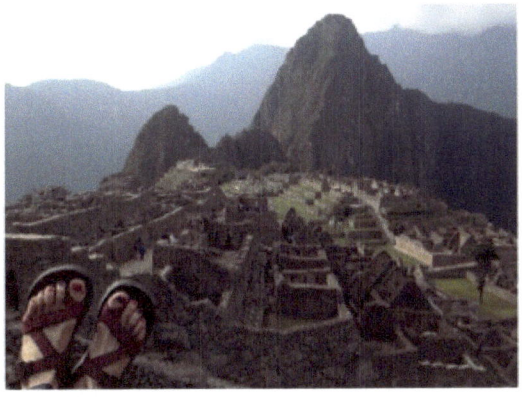

7~ Imagination has Real Psychological Effects

The creation of beneficial psychological outcomes also occurred just from imagining new "memories" in our minds. Keti's husband suffered a stroke losing many of his memories. During his recovery, he became angry and frustrated, putting their whole family on edge. After bringing him into her inner garden, Keti intuitively felt that, if he went to visit his sister and his mother, they could recount their memories of his childhood which, maybe, he would accept as his own.

It worked for him and he returned home with new memories from these discussions of his past, which he felt were his own memories. The perception of having back his memories of his earlier years changed his behavior during this recovery period from almost constant anger and frustration to a more confident and capable view of himself.

I also noticed beneficial effects when I gave myself a new memory by replacing a true event with an imaginary event. At one point, while living in Hawaii, one of my dear friends suddenly stopped returning my calls, would not talk to me, or see me. All contact was completely discontinued and the friendship was severed. Although I sought communication and understanding from my friend, there was no response, which, of course, deeply saddened me.

I went about my life and, after a couple of years of practicing *Mana Gardening*, my desire for understanding why our friendship had ended so abruptly resurfaced. Since such communication with my friend had not yet been offered, and asking for it in real life certainly didn't feel right, I decided to give myself the gift of this communication by imagining personal interaction and honesty with my friend in my inner garden.

At a lovely Hawaiian waterfall in my inner garden, I imagined a beautiful, heartfelt session with my dear friend. In my mind (or perhaps my heart), my friend communicated her honest feelings, took responsibility, and apologized sincerely for cutting off our friendship and for the effects this had on me. In this space, I also apologized for my contributions as well as any negative affects my friend experienced.

Although this experience was completely imagined, I felt the emotions of it as if it really occurred, thus changing my perspective and behavior. The next time I saw my friend around town, my behavior toward her was more compassionate, less awkward, and less emotionally charged. My personal confidence and happiness improved due to my changed perception and belief in the imagined experience of resolution.

The only thing in life we truly have the power to change is our perspective.

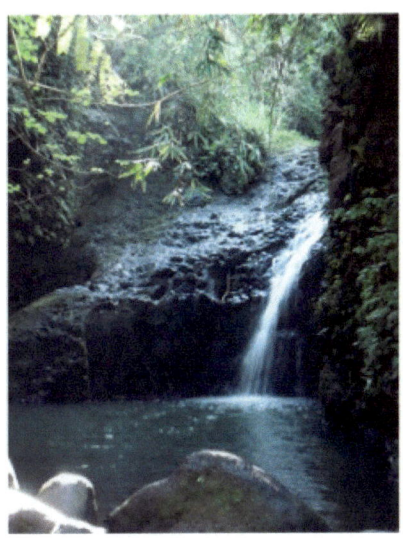

Keti and I found several scientific studies that support the idea that believing a harmless fabrication (such as creating a false memory and believing it) can change the behavior of the believer. In one study, participants tried to convince researchers that something false had in fact happened to them. As the participants told the story of the lie, they actually convinced themselves of the lie and started believing it was true as measured using various psychological assessments.[26]

Another research group examined the effects on behavior after creating false memories.[27] The participants in this study were provided with a personalized suggestion (that something occurred to them in the past) or a generalized suggestion (that something occurred to another in the past). The suggestion was either that the participant or some other person had been ill as a child from eating spoiled peach yogurt.

In taste tests one week and one month later involving many crackers and yogurts, reduced consumption of only peach yogurt was shown for those who received the personalized suggestion (that they themselves had been ill due to consuming spoiled peach yogurt). Those who believed the false memory ate the least amount of peach yogurt. This suggests that believing false memories impacts the behavior of the believer.[27]

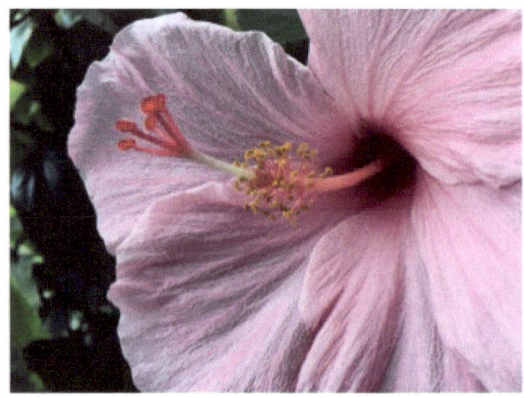

Perhaps, if you change an unbeneficial memory or experience into a more beneficial one and you start believing it, new behaviors can emerge. These studies support what Keti's husband experienced post-stroke by believing the memories from his family members and what I experienced from creating an imaginary apology and resolution experience in my garden that I believed. Keti's husband's and my behavior changed due to believing our false "memories".

What if the truth is a painful or traumatic memory? Keti and I couldn't help but wonder if this method of re-creating experiences via *Mana Gardening* can help those with memories of events that are harmful to their personal wellbeing, such as with posttraumatic stress disorder (PTSD). Perhaps imagining something better is a new way to utilize the brain to restore a healthier self-image.

Science had just begun to consider the fact that the mind could still be molded well beyond childhood when Keti and I stumbled upon this concept. Up until recently, the medical world held tight to the idea that many of our life patterns are set by age three or seven, but neuroplasticity studies are challenging this belief.

If it's possible that old thoughts, patterns, stories, and memories can be replaced throughout your entire life, *Mana Gardening* may be a far more powerful tool than we ever imagined. What if imagining new outcomes and events in your inner garden and believing them can reduce the power that unbeneficial or unresolved memories have on your personal wellbeing? What if believing the fabricated event or new experience as a memory helps neutralize old emotions and make room for new behavior and thus new creations and new life?

When I imagined in my garden a sincere, heartfelt apology with my friend, I replaced the true experience (that communication had not yet been offered) with a new experience (that my friend expressed her true feelings about ending the friendship). The effect was that I felt a sense of relief and a feeling of understanding and compassion that affected my attitude and behavior in a beneficial way.

Jerzy Konorski, in 1948, proposed that if you do not reinforce something that you have habitually reinforced, such as an old memory, and you add a new response or a replacement response, such as a new memory, or thought, you may obtain new neural reorganization that actually competes with the old memory by inhibiting it somewhat.[28] In other words, if you stop remembering an old memory, add a new thought in its place and continue to think the new thought, new neural pathways can develop that override the old memory and replace it with the new one.

This is consistent with my communication and resolution experience with my friend, where I felt an immediate shift as if the negative energy of the former memory was gone. I held on to the new perception and new compassionate behavior for several weeks.

However, I later had to go back and "re-remember" the false memory several times to maintain the new perspective, and my belief in the experience, so that I could continue to exhibit the new and beneficial behavior. This effort was, perhaps, reinforcing the new "memory" (instead of the old one) and stabilizing new neural circuitry. Perhaps we will discover that the power of our imagination, with tools such as *Mana Gardening*, can give us a way to reset our past, present, and even future.

Positive Psychological Outcomes from Changing Perceptions

Believing a harmless fabrication can change the behavior of the believer:

- *Study participants told a lie, convinced themselves and started believing it was true based on various psychological assessments[26]*

- *Spoiled peach yogurt experiment: Those who believed a negative false memory about themselves ate the least amount of peach yogurt[27]*

- *Stroke patient created and believed new memories causing him to feel more capable, reducing his anger and frustration outbursts*

- *An imagined experience of resolution caused me to feel at peace, reducing my uneasiness and trepidation around my friend*

Meet Jerzy Konorski

Jerzy Konorski, in 1948, proposed that if you do not reinforce something that you have habitually reinforced, such as an old memory, and you add a new response or a replacement response, such as a new "memory," or thought, you may obtain new neural reorganization that actually competes with the old memory by inhibiting it somewhat.[28]

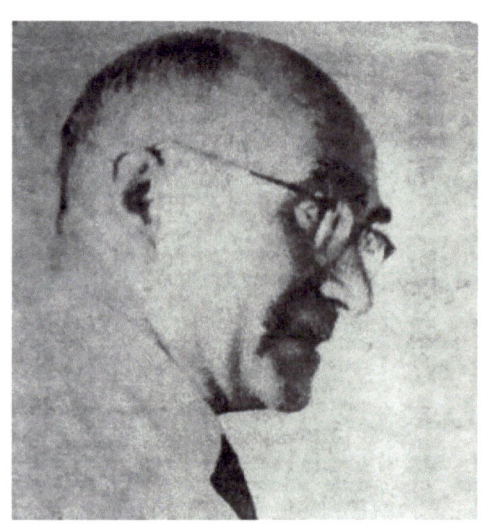

8~ The Power of Belief & the Placebo Effect

Belief is very powerful—it may be one of the most powerful forces to which we have access. The well-known placebo effect has demonstrated the power of belief repeatedly.[29-33] Although other factors are known to contribute to the placebo effect, in the classical sense, it is the conscious belief that something may be therapeutic or beneficial, leading to measurable physical improvement and the lessening of symptoms.

In medical research, this is well-documented with placebo pills, sham surgeries, and the like. Placebos, such as sugar pills, (which contain no active medicinal compounds) are given to study participants by pharmacological researchers as part of the FDA approval program to test the effectiveness of new drugs. Many times, the participants don't know whether they are getting the active drug; however, placebos repeatedly demonstrate equal effectiveness or are almost as effective as the treatment itself.[30,32,34-36]

**You don't need the medicine at all;
you just need to
BELIEVE
you have been given the medicine.**

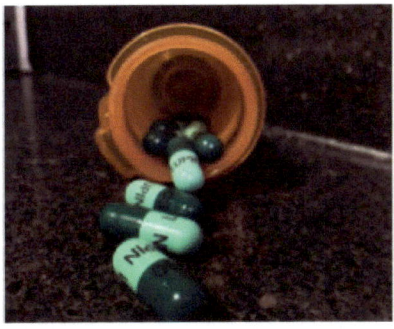

Placebos have measurable effects on people: Muscle relaxation was produced when a placebo was given as a muscle relaxant and, when described as a muscle stimulant, muscle tension was observed.[36] Intoxication[35] and sensorimotor impairment[37] can result from placebos characterized as alcohol. Compounds perceived as stimulants were shown to have stimulating effects on blood pressure and heart rhythm, and similar compounds when presented as depressants, were shown to elicit the opposite effects.[38] Substances that are not allergenic when presented to study participants as allergens can cause allergies.[34] These results highlight the importance of the patient's belief or perception in physical outcomes. Not surprisingly, the placebo effect has been shown to be related to perception and expectation.[39]

In relationship to the placebo effect, belief and perception appear to be powerful allies in one's wellbeing. In a 2007 study, neuroscientist Donald Price of the University of Florida and his colleagues used magnetic resonance imaging to scan the brains of patients with irritable bowel syndrome while they underwent a painful procedure.

Price's team showed that when patients believed they were receiving an analgesic, not only did their pain diminish, but neuronal activity also declined significantly in five pain-sensing brain regions and were identical to results in which patients were given a real painkiller.[40]

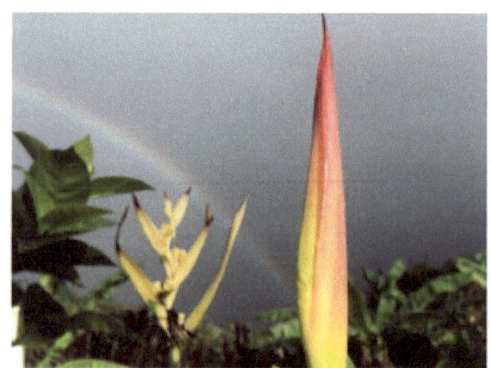

The patients believed they received painkillers when in fact they received a placebo, and their bodies and brains reacted as if they in fact had painkillers circulating in their systems. This study, and others, suggest that your brain and body believe what you believe.[32,38,40,41] Neuroscience is starting to show that your physical body and your brain react to your beliefs. Perhaps changing your beliefs through imagined wellbeing can create that wellbeing in real life.

**Your body believes you:
it reacts to whatever you believe.**

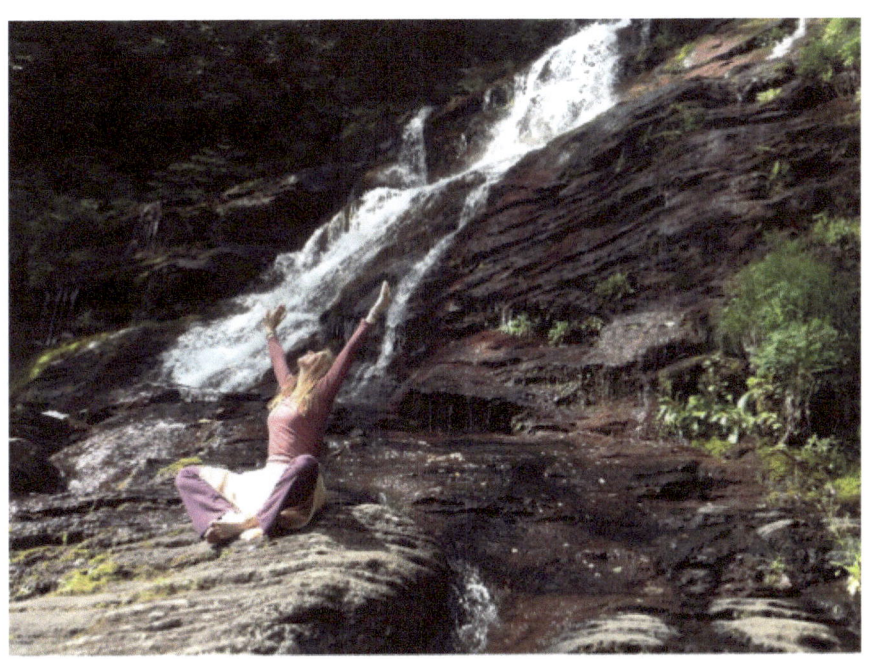

The Power of Belief & the Placebo Effect

- *The placebo effect is the conscious belief that something may be therapeutic or beneficial, leading to measurable physical improvement and the lessening of symptoms*

- *The placebo effect has demonstrated the power of belief repeatedly* [29-33]

- *Placebos continually demonstrate equal effectiveness or are almost as effective as the treatment itself* [30,32,34-36]

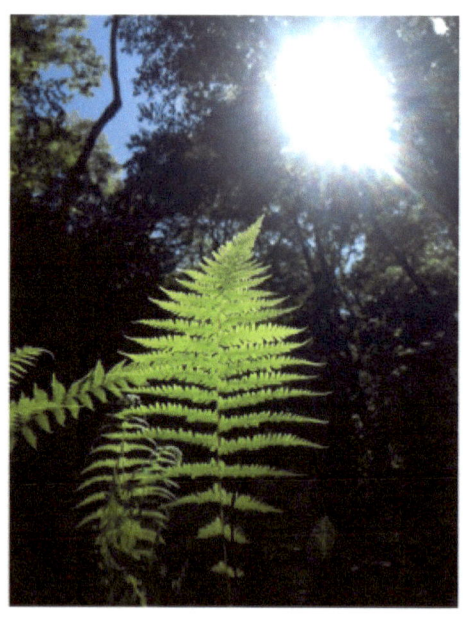

Belief & Perception = Powerful Allies

- *Price, 2007: a placebo analgesic resulted in diminished pain and significantly declined neuronal activity in five pain-sensing brain regions* [41]

- *Price, 2007: placebo results were identical to results in which patients were given a real painkiller* [41]

- *Your physical body and your brain react to your beliefs* [32,38,40,41]

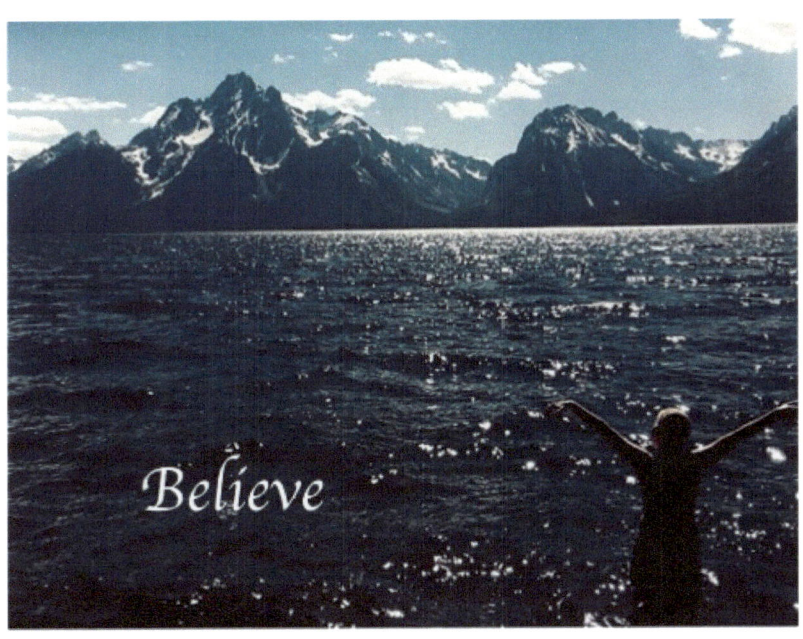

9~ Improved Intuition through Imagination

Keti and I experienced increased intuition from *Mana Gardening* with each other in a process we call Light Gardening (from chapter 6, *Mana Gardening, Empower Yourself and Live a Better Life*). Often we felt as if we were tuning into each other's feelings, emotions or heart without any conversation in real life. We had an ability to just "know" what was going on for the other or what one another may need. Often we identically started or ended one another's conversation, or started talking on the exact same topic. At other times, I spoke exactly what Keti needed to hear without a word from her. Keti was able to sense me when I wasn't around, know when I was feeling a bit off, and give me a call to guide me back to the inner garden. This holds true now that we live thousands of miles apart. It's like tapping into a stream, an untouchable field of consciousness, where information concerning one another flows.

A study involving musicians suggests increased intuition from collective mental imagery (similar to Light Gardening). This research study based on brain images and various performance endpoints suggested that when musicians imagined engaging in the musical performance piece prior to the performance, they played well together easily and the music was more cohesive. The authors of the study postulated that perhaps the musicians were tapping into intuition or predicting one another's action or timing to arrive at a more perfected performance.[42]

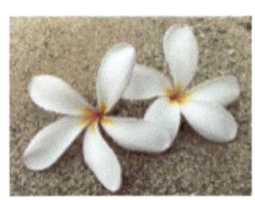

10~ Creation through Imagination

We have described scientific studies that show physical as well as psychological effects created from imagined experiences. In addition, studies show that it's possible to improve performance and intuition using imagination. What you imagine in your inner garden, you can create in real life.

Along this idea, a month or so after I created the apology and resolution experience in my inner garden with my friend, we saw each other in real life after a yoga class and she invited me to go on a hike. I gladly accepted this invitation and, on the hike, received the most openhearted, authentic communication and mutual forgiveness I have ever experienced in my life.

Among the lush foliage near a waterfall (just as in my imagined scenario), in person, we openly expressed our feelings, apologized, and forgave one another completely. Friendship renewed, we both felt as if all discordant energy from the past completely cleared from us. My imaginary communication and apology experience actually happened in real life.

Similar scenarios imagined in the context of the inner garden have also come true in real life. For example, Keti and I imagined resolution experiences with several others that have manifested in real life as well. In each case, once we imagined the experience and perceived and felt that everything was resolved, the other person initiated communication with us within 2 weeks resulting in a clearing and resolution in real life.

In another situation, Keti used her imagination to determine what was the best path for having her parents reside near her. Keti visited her inner garden, asked what she wanted, and what is the best solution for all. It was revealed that the best solution was not adding on to her house. It was for a separate dwelling that was close enough where she could check on her Dad without getting in the car, and where her Mom could have her own kitchen. She imagined this, plus a nice view from her parents' new house.

Fortuitously, a few weeks later, the neighbor offered his 3 acres of land off-market at a reasonable price, right across the street and up the hill. She discovered it had a great view. That is where she had her parent's house built.

I imagined in my inner garden a phenomenal relationship with a romantic partner. I imagined all the things we'd enjoy doing together, our open communication, both of us 100% all in, both of us 100% willing to grow together and maintain our sweet connection. I imagined our alignment, our solid commitment and trust, and our deep and fulfilling love (and much more!) This man is now in my life!

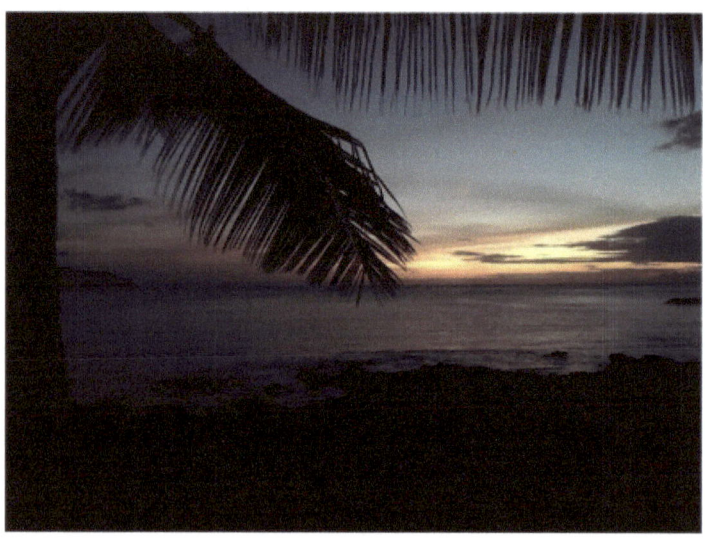

In the inner garden, Keti and I imagined sharing the wisdom of *Mana Gardening* through leading retreats and feeling the fulfillment of helping others. We have been repeatedly invited to facilitate retreats and gatherings and feel greatly fulfilled in sharing our work.

As previously mentioned, this inner garden space is creative, and imagined events have the opportunity to be actualized in real life. This, combined with feelings and belief in the imagined experience, perhaps creates new neural circuitry that establishes a "memory" that triggers magnetizes, or opens a stream of collective consciousness that allows these experiences to manifest in real life.

**What you imagine on the inside
can be created on the outside,
in real life.**

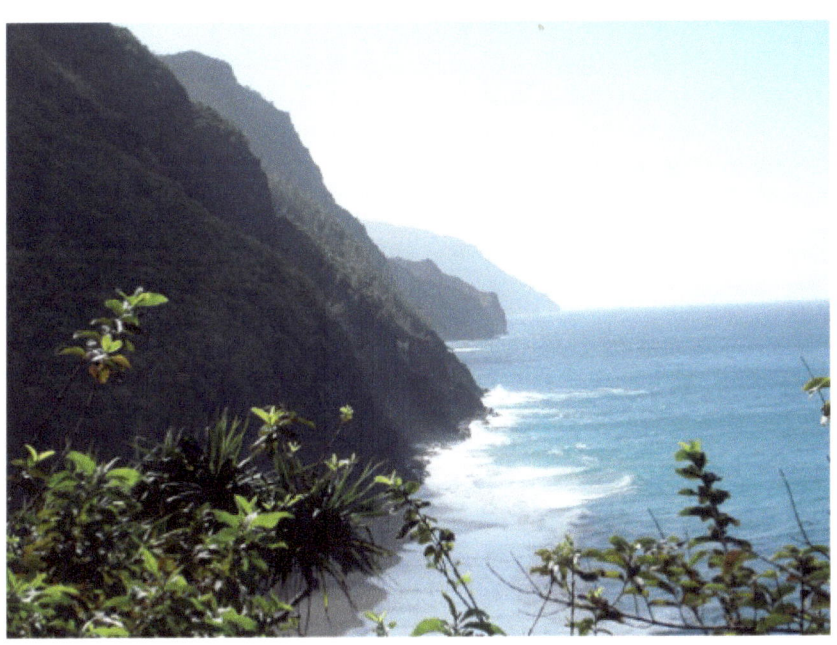

11~ Conclusion: You Are A Powerful Creator!

Data from studies of the powerful effects of imagination presented here support the idea that what you imagine, believe, or perceive to be true is *real* on both biological and psychological levels. Brain stimulation, measurable physical effects in the body, neurological reorganization, as well as behavioral changes have been documented based on imaginary events.

Studies in motor imagery (simulated or imaginary exercise) showed that the body actually responds to the thoughts and actions of the mind or imagination. Studies also revealed that the kinesthetic (sensory/feeling) investment is a vital link to neurological reorganization. Psychological benefits are also possible using processes such as *Mana Gardening*—if a perception can become a belief that creates a changed behavior and measurable changes in the body and brain, then we hold immense generative power through the use of our imaginations. There is ample scientific evidence to support what we have found for ourselves, that...

Your imagination is powerful beyond measure and you can use it to create changes that will help you live a better life!

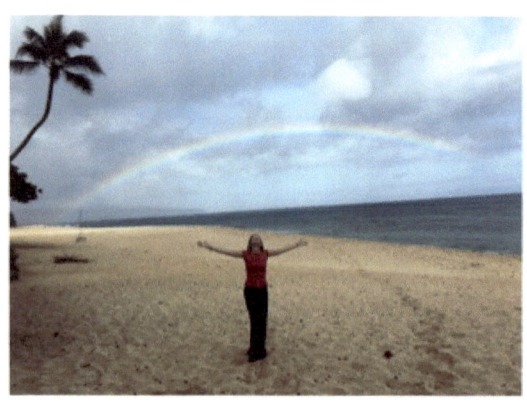

12~ Guided Meditation: Imagine Your Sacred Inner Garden

Let's do some *Mana Gardening*. What is heaven to you? What would constitute your idea of a sacred paradise where all your needs and desires are met? A place or space where you feel nurtured, completely accepted and loved unconditionally? Close your eyes and visualize this. Put yourself there, in that scene. Allow your shoulders to sink down and breathe deeply. Feel a few seconds or minutes of relief and relaxation. Allow absolutely NO negativity or anything that could disrupt your peace in this scene whatsoever. Any time you have more than 15 seconds of free time, do this again. Imagine your inner paradise and bask in that feeling of instant relief from everyone and everything. And feel the wellbeing and *Mana* flowing.

Every time you give yourself the gift of this experience, you are changing your perspective, biology and health in a positive way. For free audio versions of *Mana Gardening* guided meditations, please visit www.ManaGardening.com.

Visualize your idea of paradise and allow yourself to be there.

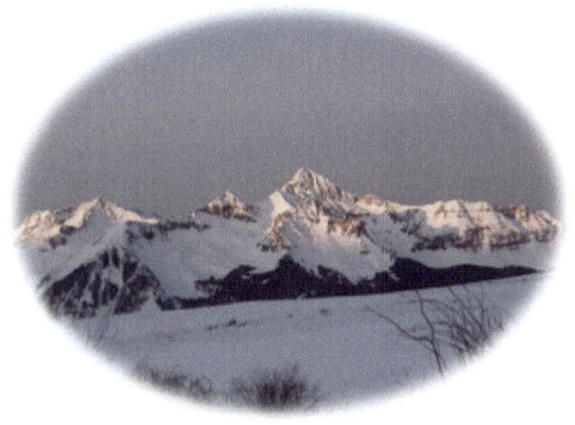

Ways *Mana Gardening* Contributes to Health & Wellbeing

- *Visualizing and feeling wellbeing and fulfillment by basking in your personal, imagined sanctuary*

- *Imaginary exercising*

- *Imagining improved performance of tasks and activities*

- *Imagining traumatic issues resolved*

- *Imaginary role play of forgiveness and communication*

- *Giving love to yourself and your body using your imagination*

- *Changes your perception giving you belief and confidence in the imagined events which may affect your biology and/or behavior in a beneficial way*

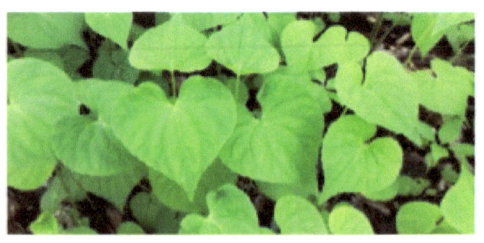

References

1. Malouin F, Richards CL, Durand A, et al. Effects of practice, visual loss, limb amputation and disuse on motor imagery vividness. *Neurorehabil Neural Repair*. 2009; 23:449–463.

2. Guillot A, Collet C, Nguyen VA, Malouin F, Richards C, et al. Brain activity during visual versus kinesthetic imagery: an fMRI study. *Hum Brain Mapp*. 2009;30: 2157–2172.

3. Guillot A, Collet C, Nguyen VA, Malouin F, Richards C, et al. Functional neuroanatomical networks associated with expertise in motorimagery. *Neuroimage*. 2008;41:1471–1483.

4. Mihara M, Miyai I, Hattori N, Hatakenaka M, Yagura H, Kawano T, Okibayashi M, Danjo N, Ishikawa A, Inoue Y, Kubota K. Neurofeedback using real-time near-infraredspectroscopy enhances motor imagery related cortical activation. *PLoS One*. 2012;7(3):e32234.

5. Ruby P, Decety J Effect of subjective perspective taking during simulation of action: a PET investigation of agency. *Nat Neurosci*. 2001;4:546–550.

6. Gerardin E, Sirigu A, Lehericy S, Poline JB, Gaymard B, et al. Partially overlapping neural networks for real and imagined hand movements. *Cereb Cortex*. 2000;10:1093–1104.

7. deCharms RC, Christoff K, Glover GH, Pauly JM, Whitfield S, et al. Learned regulation of spatially localized brain activation using real-time fMRI. *Neuroimage*. 2004;21:436–443.

References

8. Lotze M, Halsband U. Motor imagery. *J Physiol Paris*. 2006;99:386–395. 9. Lotze M, Halsband U. Motor imagery. *J Physiol Paris*. 2006;99:386–395.

9. Malouin F, Richards CL. Mental practice for relearning locomotor skills. *Phys Ther*. 2010;90(2):240-51.

10. Malouin F, Richards CL, Jackson PL, et al. Brain activations during motor imagery of locomotor-related tasks: a PET study. *Hum Brain Mapp*. 2003;19:47–62.

11. Subramian L, Morris MB, Brosnan M, Turner DL, Morris HR, Linden DE. Functional magnetic resonance imaging neurofeedback-guided motor imagery training and motor training for Parkinson's disease: randomized trial. *Front Behave Neurosci*. 2016;10–111.

12. Marins TF, Rodrigues EC, Engel A, et al. Enhancing motor network activity using real-time functional MRI neurofeedback of left premotor cortex. *Front Behav Neurosci*. 2015; 9:341.

13. Szameitat AJ, Shen S, Sterr A. Motor imagery of complex everyday movements: an fMRI study. *Neuroimage*. 2007;34:702–713.

14. Jackson PL, Lafleur MF, Malouin F, et al. Potential role of mental practice using motor imagery in neurological rehabilitation. *Arch Phys Med Rehabil*. 2001;82:1133–1141.

15. Decety J, Perani D, Jeannerod M, Bettinardi V, Tadary B, et al. Mapping motor representations with positron emission tomography. *Nature*. 1994;371:600–602.

References

16. Decety J, Jeannerod M, Germain M, Pastene J. Vegetative responses during imagined movement is proportional to mental effort. *Behav Brain Res.* 1991:42:1–5.

17. Wuyam B, Moosavi SH, Decety J, et al. Imagination of dynamic exercise produced ventilatory responses which were more apparent in competitive sportsmen. *J Physiol.* 1995;482:713–724.

18. Fusi S, Cutuli D, Valente MR, et al. Cardioventilatory responses during real or imagined walking at low speed. *Arch Ital Biol.* 2005;143:223–228.

19. Sacco K, Cauda F, Cerliani L, et al. Motor imagery of walking following training in locomotor attention: the effect of "the tango lesson." *Neuroimage.* 2006;32:1441–1449.

20. Dickstein R, Deutsch JE. Motor imagery in physical therapist practice. *Phys Ther.* 2007;87:942–953.

21. Slimani M, Taylor L, Baker JS, Elleuch A, et al. Effects of mental training on muscular force, hormonal and physiological changes in kickboxers. *J Sports Med Phys Fitness.* 2016 Jul 5.

22. Murphy SM. Imagery interventions in sport. *Med Sci Sports Exerc.* 1994;26:486–494.

23. Guillot A, Moschberger K, Collet C. Coupling movement with imagery as a new perspective for motor imagery practice. *Behav Brain Funct.* 2013;Feb 20;9(1):8.

References

24. Moran A, Guillot A, Macintyre T, Collet C. Re-imagining motor imagery: building bridges between cognitive neuroscience and sport psychology. *Br J Psychol.* 2012;103(2):224-47.

25. Anema HA, de Haan AM, Gebuis T, Dijkerman HC. Thinking about touch facilitates tactile but not auditory processing. *Exp Brain Res.* 2012; 218(3):373-80.

26. Polage DC. Fabrication inflation increases as source monitoring ability decreases. *Acta Psychol.* 2012;139(2):335-42.

27. Scoboria A, Mazzoni G, Jarry JL, Bernstein DM. Personalized and not general suggestion produces false autobiographical memories and suggestion-consistent behavior. *Acta Psychol.* 2012;139(1):225-32.

28. Konorski J. Conditioned Reflexes and Neuron Organization. Cambridge: Cambridge University Press. (1948) p 134.

29. Kaptchuk TJ, Friedlander E, Kelley JM, Sanchez MN, et al. Placebos without Deception: A Randomized Controlled Trial in Irritable Bowel Syndrome. *PLoS ONE.* 2010;5 (12):e15591.

30. Miller FG, Colloca L, Kaptchuk TJ. The placebo effect: illness and interpersonal healing. *Perspec Biol Med.* 2009;52:518–39.

31. Flik CE, Bakker L, Laan W, vaan Rood YR, et al. Systematic Review: The placebo effect of psychological interventions in the treatment of irritable bowel syndrome. *World J Gastroenterol.* 2017:23(12):2223-2233.

References

32. Benson H, McCallie DP. Angina pectoris and the placebo effect. *N Engl J of Med.* 1979;300 (25):1424–9.

33. Moseley JB, O'Malley K, Petersen NJ, et al. "A controlled trial of arthroscopic surgery for osteoarthritis of the knee". *N Engl J of Med.* 2002;347 (2): 81–8.

34. Ikemi Y, Nakagawa S. A psychosomatic study of contagious dermatitis. *Kyoshu J Med Sci* 1962;13:335–50.

35. O'Boyle DJ, Binns AS, Sumner JJ. On the efficacy of alcohol placebos in inducing feelings of intoxication. *Psychopharmacol.* 1994;115 (1–2):229–36.

36. Flaten MA, Simonsen T, Olsen H. Drug-related information generates placebo and nocebo responses that modify the drug response. *Psychosom Med.* 1999;61 (2):250–5.

37. Fillmore MT, Mulvihill LE, Vogel-Sprott M. "The expected drug and its expected effect interact to determine placebo responses to alcohol and caffeine". *Psychopharmacol.* 1994;115(3):383–8.

38. Kirsch I. Specifying non-specifics: Psychological mechanism of the placebo effect. The Placebo Effect: An Interdisciplinary Exploration. Cambridge: Harvard University Press. (1997) p. 166–86.

39. Buckalew LW, Ross S. Relationship of perceptual characteristics to efficacy of placebos. *Psychol Rep.* 1981;49 (3):955–61.

References

40. Price DD, Craggs J, Verne GN, Perlstein WM, Robinson ME. Placebo analgesia is accompanied by large reductions in pain-related brain activity in irritable bowel syndrome patients. *Pain*. 2007;127(1-2):63-72.

41. Kirsch I, Weixel LJ. Double-blind versus deceptive administration of a placebo. *Behav Neurosci*. 1988;102(2):319-323.

42. Keller PE. Mental imagery in music performance: underlying mechanisms and potential benefits. *Ann N Y Acad Sci*. 2012;1252:206-13.

Michelle Shine, Ph.D. and Keti Kamalani are dedicated to sharing the ancient Hawaiian wisdom of *Mana Gardening*. They are available for seminars, conferences, workshops, book signing, webinars, interviews, retreats and private sessions. *Mana Gardening* training is available online, via teleconference and in-person.

Mana Gardening Institute, LLC is a woman-owned, Hawaii-based organization established to facilitate scientific research in forthright personal empowerment and *Mana Gardening* techniques. Visit the website to learn more about Mana Sciences[TM] and Mana Psychology[TM] research and follow us on Facebook/Twitter/Instagram under Mana Gardening.

www.ManaGardening.com

GET MANA and be EMPOWERED

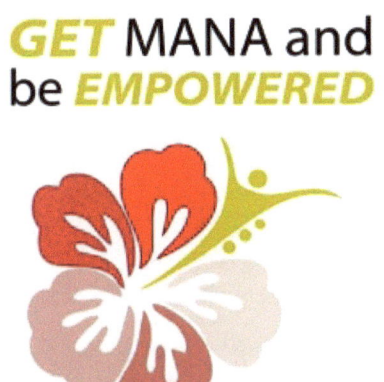

The Hawaiian empowerment techniques communicated in this guidebook are described in detail with real life experiences from the authors as well as scientific references in our book, *Mana Gardening, Empower Yourself and Live a Better Life*.

This widely available, full-length, easy-to-read book guides you into progressively deeper aspects of using your imagination to create what you want to experience. Readers have professed that this body of work is, "Groundbreaking and profound!"

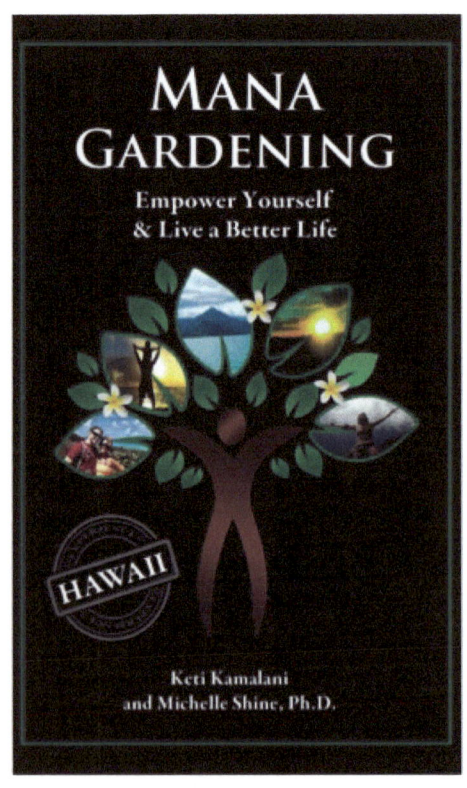

www.ingramcontent.com/pod-product-compliance
Lightning Source LLC
Chambersburg PA
CBHW040250220526
45473CB00001B/430